The Moral Warrior

SUNY series, Ethics and the Military Profession
George R. Lucas Jr., editor

The Moral Warrior

Ethics and Service in the U.S. Military

Martin L. Cook

STATE UNIVERSITY OF NEW YORK PRESS

Fo Blkwl. 6/08 22.05

Published by
State University of New York Press, Albany

For information, contact State University of New York Press, Albany, NY
www.sunypress.edu

Production by Diane Ganeles
Marketing by Anne M. Valentine

Library of Congress Cataloging-in-Publication Data

Cook, Martin L., 1951–
    The moral warrior : ethics and service in the U.S. military / Martin L. Cook.
        p. cm. — (SUNY series, ethics and the military profession)
    Includes bibliographical references and index.
    ISBN 0–7914–6241–2 (hc.: alk. paper) — ISBN 0–7914–6242–0 (pbk.: alk.
    paper)
    1. Military ethics—United States. 2. United States—Military policy—
    Moral and ethical aspects. 3. United States—Armed Forces—Moral and
    ethical aspects. I. Title. II. Series.

U22.C597 2004
172´.42´0973—dc22

2003068709

10 9 8 7 6 5

KING HENRY. . . . methinks I could not die anywhere so contented as in the King's company, his cause being just and his quarrel honourable.

WILLIAMS. That's more than we know.

BATES. Ay, or more than we should seek after; for we know enough if we know we are the King's subjects. If his cause be wrong, our obedience to the King wipes the crime of it out of us.

WILLIAMS. But if the cause be not good, the King himself hath a heavy reckoning to make when all those legs and arms and heads, chopp'd off in a battle ... I am afeard there are few die well that die in a battle; for how can they charitably dispose of anything when blood is their argument? Now, if these men do not die well, it will be a black matter for the King that led them to it ....

KING HENRY. So, if a son that is by his father sent about merchandise do sinfully miscarry upon the sea, the imputation of his wickedness, by your rule, should be imposed upon his father that sent him.... But this is not so: the King is not bound to answer the particular endings of his soldiers ... for they purpose not their death when they purpose their services. Besides, there is no king, be his cause never so spotless, if it come to the arbitrement of swords, can try it out with all unspotted soldiers....

—*Henry V*, act 4, scene 1

Contents

Preface

The role, nature, and conduct of the military of the United States are subjects worthy of deep reflection at this juncture in American history. Although our military operates largely out of sight of many of our citizens and even of our leaders much of the time, our military and its role in the world is changing, and the military itself is rapidly evolving along several axes.

Never in American history have we maintained a large all-volunteer (or, perhaps better, all-recruited) military force. In the past, the American military demobilized to very small forces in peacetime and then conscripted forces when large numbers were required for the next major conflict. This is itself a dramatic change in our military. On the one hand, America's military is much more professional, better trained and equipped, and of higher quality than we have ever experienced. On the other hand, unlike large conscripted forces, it is unrepresentative of the society it serves in many respects and, some fear, deeply alienated from that society. For many, our military has become a family business as more and more of its members, especially of the officer corps, are themselves products of military families. Politically, America's military (and especially the officer corps) is overwhelming Republican in its politics. Both of these developments raise concern, if not alarm. Concepts of apolitical military professionalism and service to the whole of American society require rearticulation and reexamination in these changed circumstances.

In parallel with those social developments in the military, there have been dramatic changes in the technology with which that military is equipped. Precision munitions in more and more weapons systems radically change the moral symmetry of risk in combat. Unmanned platforms are rapidly proliferating that alter that symmetry even further. Electronic communications, satellite imagery, and computer technology provide a comprehensive awareness of the battlefield and work together to make the US military effective in ways no other military on the planet can even approximate. These developments raise new ethical questions about the appropriate use and limits of such capabilities. Each new development raises questions, many of them unforeseen, about the limits and proper use of those systems.

Cumulatively, these evolutionary changes in the role and nature of our military make the United States the sole remaining superpower (or, if one prefers, "hyperpower") on the planet. This fact, too, raises fundamental questions about the international system and the role of the United States in it. How, for example, do we combine the reality of American uniqueness with the concept of sovereign equality of states that forms the bedrock of the Westphalian international system and the United Nations? Especially in the Global War on Terrorism (GWOT) in which we are now engaged, how do rules of international relations accommodate the twin realities of American uniqueness and having an adversary that does not take the form of a state?

This book is an exploration of many dimensions of these issues.

Acknowledgments

This book is grounded not only in research and scholarship, but also in the privilege of working and teaching for five years at the United States Army War College, Carlisle Barracks, Pennsylvania. America's war colleges help to prepare our military's most senior leaders. The outstanding men and women who advance to the rank of lieutenant colonel and colonel are indeed an elite community of professionals. Without the benefit of constant learning from their vast accumulated experience and knowledge, a book like this would be impossible for a civilian scholar to write. It is appropriately dedicated to my esteemed colleagues and former students at the Army War College.

As I complete this manuscript, many of my former students are returning from or deploying to positions of command in Iraq and Afghanistan. My respect for their dedication, professionalism, courage, and sacrifice is unbounded.

Earlier versions of the following chapters appeared originally in the following publications with whose permission they are used here. Grateful acknowledgment is made to them. The Introduction was modified from an essay originally published as "On Being a Sole Remaining Superpower: Lessons from History," *Journal of Military Ethics* (v. 1, Issue 2), 2002, 77–90, and is used here by permission of Taylor & Francis AS. Chapter 2 was modified from an essay originally published as "Why Serve the State? Moral Foundations of Military Officership." *The Leader's Imperative: Ethics, Integrity and Responsibility*, J. Carl Ficarrotta, ed. (West Lafayette, IN: Purdue University Press, 2001). Chapter 3 was modified from an essay originally published as "Army Professionalism: Service to What Ends?" *The Future of the Army Profession*, Don M. Snider and Gayle L. Watkins, eds. (Boston: McGraw-Hill Primus, 2002), 337-354. Chapter 4 was modified from an essay originally published as "The Proper Role of Professional Military Advice in Contemporary Uses of Military Force," *Parameters*, v. XXXII, n. 4 (Winter 2002–2003), 21–33. Chapter 5 was modified from an essay originally published as "Just Peacemaking: Challenges of Humanitarian Intervention," *Journal of the Society of Christian Ethics* (v. 23, n. 1), 241–253. Chapter 7 was modified from an essay originally published as "Immaculate War: Constraints on Humanitarian Intervention." *Ethics and International Affairs*, 14(2000), 55–65. Chapter 8 was modified from an essay originally published as "Strategic Theory, Military Practice, and the Laws of War: The Case of Strategic Bombing," in Anthony F. Lang, Albert C. Pierce, and Joel H. Rosenthal, eds., *Ethics and the Future of Conflict: Lessons from the 1990s* (Upper Saddle River, NJ: Prentice Hall, Inc., 2003), 163–182. Chapter 9 was modified from an essay originally published as "Two Roads Diverged, and We Took the One Less Traveled: Just Recourse to War and the Kosovo Intervention." *Kosovo: Contending Voice on the Balkan Intervention*, William Buckley, ed. (Grand Rapids: Eerdmans Press, 2000).

Dr. George Lucas of the United States Naval Academy and editor of this series in military ethics for SUNY Press has been a loyal friend and constant encouragement during the compilation of this work. I speak truly when I say that, without his efforts, this book would not have been produced.

Lastly, but most importantly, I want to acknowledge and express gratitude for the love and support of my wife, Birgitta Gustafson, and Aliya and Laila, my daughters. The loving home they helped provide was in every way conducive to scholarly productivity. Birgitta, in addition to encouragement, applied her critical expertise to every page of the manuscript—itself a work of love.

Introduction

The Sole Remaining Superpower

Imagine this scenario: For fifty years, a grand voluntary alliance of independent states has held the line against an imperial expansionist state that has swallowed all in its path up to the alliance's border. The hegemonic intentions of this state have been held in check by a few crucial victories of the alliance.

The defensive alliance began as an association of independent and relatively equal states united in a defense pact. Each member state, in proportion to its economic and political power, contributed to the defense against the common threat.

But over the decades, as the threat to the alliance grew less palpable, fewer and fewer member states were willing voluntarily to allocate the physical resources necessary to keep their fighting capability high. Nor were they willing to spend the money needed to preserve the alliance's credibility and high state of readiness.

In the face of a general distaste for alliance adventures, one state took the lead. It argued for a large, rapidly deployable, and highly mobile force, capable of quickly meeting any hostile actions directed at the alliance. It alone maintained the political will to maintain such a force in being and a unified command structure prepared for any contingency that might arise.

As her allies abdicated responsibility for collective security, this state grew from being a "first among equals" to being the sole major power. Increasingly, other member states of the alliance preferred to make their contribution by granting basing rights to the leading state.

The smaller states found these basing support arrangements for the major power more palatable to their political systems than sustaining the trained and ready fighting units from their own states that had been the foundation of the alliance in its earlier form.

Initially happy to be freed of the burden of sustaining their own forces, the lesser states of the alliance came to place all their reliance on the military might of the sole remaining superpower. In the unlikely event that the distant hegemon should once again threaten the region, or that small-scale emergencies should arise in the alliance's area of responsibility, the alliance superpower's military would cope with the problem. For all parties, this "arrangement of convenience" seemed for a time to be acceptable all around.

As the superpower grew and the member states waned in capability, the superpower was more and more in a position not merely to receive the voluntary support of the member states, but increasingly to pressure, and finally to demand and coerce, coalition support for its military power. But, the superpower felt justified even in the coercion of former allies, for she sincerely believed that she alone correctly perceived the threat and that her actions genuinely served the common good of the alliance.

Visitors to the superpower's territories from alliance states could not but perceive its growing economic superiority and dominance; they could not miss the growing gap in wealth and cultural dominance of the superpower over their world. Money contributed for common defense was used to build public buildings of great grandeur in the superpower, and supported its vital cultural and artistic life (exported, with increasing resentment, throughout the alliance's territory).

One traditionally difficult alliance member began to complain that the gap between the superpower and all her former allies was approaching a point of no return. Unless something was done, and done soon, the superpower would emerge as the absolute and incontestably dominant power in their world as far into the future as the eye could see.

Eventually, sparked by agitation by this state, a segment of the old alliance came to see the superpower itself as the major threat to the peace and independence of the member states. While the potential threat of the old hegemon lurked in the background, the daily reality of the superpower's increasingly imperious demands was clear and present. Indeed, from the allies' perspective, her demands seemed to grow in inverse proportion to the visibility of the threat.

The scenario just sketched is, of course, the summary of the growing power of Athens in the lull following the Persian Wars. The events set the stage for the war with the former allies of Athens, the Peloponnesian League. It incited the struggles among the allies of Athens, the Delian League, and the war between the Delian League and a resurgent alliance centered on Sparta, events narrated in that classic military history and strategy, the history of the Peloponnesian War by the Athenian historian Thucydides.

While there were many small incidents and provocations leading to the war, its great chronicler, Thucydides, reduced them to one: "The growth of the power of Athens, and the alarm which this inspired in Sparta, made war inevitable" (1.23.5).[1] Thucydides wrote his work to be "a possession for all time," and indeed it is.

Any resemblance between that scenario and the situation of the United States and NATO following the withdrawal of the Soviet Union from the world stage is far from coincidental.

The conduct of Athens toward her former allies, her supreme confidence that she faced no peer in the foreseeable future, and her strategic and operational blunders once a segment of her former allies took up arms against her combined to bring about her utter destruction.

Far too often, when Thucydides' work is taught at all in professional military education or in standard political science and international relations courses, it is taught extremely superficially. How many times has the Melian Dialogue, ripped completely from its context, been used merely to illustrate "realism" as a theory of international relations?

The full richness of A History of the Peloponnesian War can only be appreciated by means of a thorough reading of the work, which follows events from the rise of Athens to imperial power to its final catastrophic fall, in many ways at her own hand. In that larger reading, the Melian Dialogue is but a cautionary tale to show how an imperial power can overplay its hand.

Thucydides' History is a classical Greek tragedy of tragic flaws and hubris. Athens plays the protagonist and the Melian protest of the injustice of her action is equivalent to the chorus in a

Sophoclean play, warning the protagonist of the folly and danger of the course she has set for herself. From the perspective of one knowing of the whole sweep of the war, the Melians were, in fact, giving wise strategic counsel and realistic advice for the long term. They argued for commonly accepted and fair international standards of action, observed by all, even by the strong.

The story of the fall of Athens can illuminate much about the besetting sins and temptations inherent in being the sole remaining superpower in the world. Indeed, this book will argue that Athens and her conduct during the period of her ascendancy form a parallel narrative well worth pondering in our own present historical circumstances. This historical analogue may provide insight into the predictable temptations of unmatched power in periods of low-intensity strategic rivalry.

The Roots of Athenian Ascendancy

Athens did not set out to be the superpower in her world. The defeat of the Persians in 490 BCE, and again in 480–479 BCE, had been accomplished by a Panhellenic alliance, that combine the renowned Spartan skill at land warfare and leadership, with Athenian naval prowess. The conclusion of that war left the Greek alliance deployed over vast stretches of the Mediterranean and united in the Delian League through voluntary contributions to a fund for the common defense at the sacred island of Delos.

The deep and widely held cultural commitment to the polis, the autonomous city-state, as the foundation of Greek society was a barrier to maintaining unity over such wide-ranging territory. Even Athens, although she was dominant over many other city-states, seemed never to conceive of forming coherent political institutions commensurate with the scope of her power. From the beginning to the end of the conflict, Athenians thought of themselves purely in terms of loyalty to their city. Other cities were thought of either as allies, enemies, or providers of tribute. The other Greek cities shared Athens's love for the particular political unit of the polis with equal enthusiasm.

At the conclusion of the Persian War, the alliance was still led by Sparta. The alliance asked Athens to lead it however, when the

Spartan king Pausanias disgraced himself in command by his arrogance and his favoritism toward the Spartan troops in the alliance.[2]
Sparta quickly reverted to her conservative ways and pulled back to
tend to her own city and traditions. Athens, by contrast, had a vast
navy, and remained engaged in both military and economic terms
with the entire Mediterranean area accessible by sea. Athenian
wealth depended on freedom of navigation and trade, and
Athenian naval power was necessary for the maintenance of both.
The successor alliance to that formed to defeat the Persians, the
Delian League, emerged with Athens at its head.

Thus did Athens become the undisputed head and leader of
the Mediterranean world. Only the loosely structured Peloponnesian "league" remained outside, and it was weakly organized and
hardly a match for the growing power of Athens.[3]

Although the Delian League was initially a voluntary alliance
and, conducted business by voting of the member states, Athens
quickly came to dominate it. Finally, in 454/453 BCE, the pretense
of equality among the states was dropped entirely. The treasury
moved from Delos to Athens, and Athens claimed one sixtieth of
the annual income of the fund for her own use—funds that were
used to build the magnificent buildings of Athens and to pay citizens for public service.

Athens had stumbled upon an empire. Ironically, having fought
for the independence of the Greek city-states in the face of the
forthrightly imperial power of Persia, Athens herself took up the
model of empire and recipient of tribute payment from subordinate
states. So having fought for the independence of the Greeks from
imperial tyranny, she herself came to play Persia's role—but without
the political system to administer an empire effectively. Indeed,
although the scope of the strategic demands of Athens was imperial, one may question whether an affiliation of nominally independent cities could ever achieve the unity required for Athens's
strategic purposes.

While still mouthing the national values of democratic government, open and tolerant social practices, and the flourishing of
the arts and sciences through unfettered thought and exploration,
Athens increasingly had to play the role of oppressor. As the
Athenians said of themselves, "That empire we acquired, not by
violence, but because you [Spartans] were unwilling to prosecute

to its conclusion the war against the barbarian, and because the allies attached themselves to us and spontaneously asked us to assume command" (1.75).

Athenians were quite capable of self-delusion about their geopolitical situation, and believed that the beauty and cultural achievements of their city and its democratic institutions justified its superior status. Because of their pride in their city's accomplishments, they were tempted to exempt themselves from ordinary standards of fairness, or even consistency with their own espoused values. But it was the hero of Thucydides' tale, Pericles, who would tell Athens the unvarnished truth: "[W]hat you hold is, to speak somewhat plainly, a tyranny; to take it perhaps was wrong, but to let it go is unsafe" (2.63.2).

Following Pericles' death early in the developing war between Athens and the Peloponnesian alliance of states centered on Sparta, the political leadership of Athens became less and less sure. Athens lost the coherent strategic vision Pericles had provided, overextended herself in too many theaters of conflict, and missed opportunities for favorable peace settlements through foolish pride after successes. Finally, catastrophically, Athens committed vast resources to a failed attempt to take and control Sicily and experienced a military defeat from which she never fully recovered.

All parties attempted to augment their power by deals with the Persians; and, while the Spartan alliance "won" the war in the short run, it meant the end of Greek civilization as it had flourished in the classical period. It was replaced by the period of true empires: the Persian empire, then the Hellenistic empire under Alexander the Great and his successors, and finally and most lastingly, the Roman Empire.

So in less than a hundred years, Athens and all of Greece went from the glory of defeating the Persians at Marathon and Salamis to the disgrace of seeing the destruction of her form of life. The art, literature, and philosophy that form the foundation of Western civilization are products of that "one brief shining moment" of Athenian ascendancy. The failure of Athens to understand and manage her strategic situation in this period led to her own destruction and opened the way to a new age of imperial conquest by other civilizations.

Was this historical course inevitable? Could Athens have used her unprecedented political and military status in the Greek world to create a more fortunate outcome? Are there lessons from Athenian experience that make Thucydides' painstaking chronicle of the demise of Athens truly the "possession for all time" (1.22) he intended? What are the lessons for grand strategy one can gain from reflection on Athens's historical experience?

In the next sections of this chapter, I will attempt to extract the main themes and blunders Thucydides' history points up as predictable traps for major powers at the height of their supremacy.

Don't Make Your Own Enemies

Athens emerged from the Persian War as a heroic and honored member of the Greek world. With astonishing boldness and courage, Athenians had abandoned their city en masse to Persian occupation and set sail for Salamis, where they decisively defeated the Persian fleet and forced Persian withdrawal. As we have already seen, after the disgrace of the Spartan Pausanias, the Athenians were invited by their allies to take the lead of the Delian League.

In the period following, Athens planted colonies throughout the Mediterranean and used her fleet to ensure the safety of a far-flung trading network that brought Greece to a new level of prosperity and peace. Athenian culture and learning flourished, making this short period of her history one of the pivotal moments in the development of human culture. Socrates and Plato, Sophocles and Euripides, Phidias and Pericles walked her streets and gave Western culture the foundations for learning and government of which we are still the heirs.

How, then, were they able so to alienate their former allies that within fifty years, the representatives of many Greek cities would meet and perceive Athens herself as their greatest threat? How can such cultural and political triumph sow the seeds of its own destruction? The conduct of Athens echoes of U.S. conduct in the current conflict:

> [W]e must ask how the coalition that Secretary of State Powell has been skillfully building is being seen by his colleagues in the government. Do they see it as a partnership in which our allies will not only provide various forms of

support, but also take part in the major decisions? As often before in NATO, the danger is that we will look at our allies as junior partners in our firm, asked to supplement our forces and to pay for the common good.[4]

The naval power of Athens—both her own forces and those she commanded by means of the Delian League—was superior, not only to her nearest rivals individually, but to all of the rest of Greece collectively. The Peloponnesian alliance had only Corinth as a major maritime power and fell far short of the Delian League's unity of command and control.[5]

As a trading nation, however, much of that power was used to prevent piracy and to maintain freedom of navigation that was very much to the benefit of all of maritime Greece. Properly used, therefore, Athenian military superiority might well have worked for the common good of Greece, and Athens may be somewhat forgiven for seeing its power in those terms, even as other cities came to resent and then fear it. Good strategic leadership might well have found a way for Athens to emerge as the natural and commonly accepted leader of an expanding and ever more prosperous Greek civilization embracing the whole of the Mediterranean world.

But Athens found ways of pursuing ever-greater superiority that could only inspire fear and suspicion in other states. The main and most natural axis of Athenian expansion and dominance was, of course, to the east. For many years, Athens was indeed content to colonize and dominate the islands and coast of the eastern Mediterranean—a large area that gave it plenty of scope for virtually indefinite expansion.

The other significant naval power in the Greek world, Corinth, had its own sphere of influence and navigation on the western side of the Greek world and along the sea lanes to Italy and Sicily. Not content with this traditional and somewhat natural division, Athens began to make encroachments that Corinth could not fail to find threatening. First, it succeeded in removing Megara from the Spartan alliance, garrisoned it, and built long walls that made its ports virtually immune to attack. Then it fortified a base at Naupactus settled by refugees from conflict with Sparta. The net effect of these moves was to place Athens in the position to threaten dominance of the

Crisaean Gulf, Corinth's access lane to the sea. As Thucydides remarks, "This was the principal cause of the Corinthians conceiving such a deadly hatred against Athens" (1.103[4]).

Needless to say, Athens perceived its actions not as threats to the security of Corinth or any other state, but merely as part of an indefinite and in principle limitless strategy of expanding empire and security arrangements. Her moves seemed to her natural and perhaps even for the common good of Greece in giving her access of the western part of the Greek world and, potentially, access to alternative sources of grain, including grain exports from Sicily.

Her pursuit of unilateral military dominance and economic self-sufficiency, however, inevitably was perceived as aggressive, and as a threat to other states' vested economic and strategic interests. It may be true, of course, that at the moment of its expansion Athens possessed the strength to make these moves with relative impunity. But as Thucydides tells us, that impunity was only of a short-term nature and created the animosity that would ripen into Corinthian agitation for rearmament and formation of an alliance of sufficient strength to oppose and contain Athenian expansion. Athens's limitless pursuit of absolute and unilateral security was the seedbed of absolute insecurity. It inevitably generated its own "arms race," as other states strove to resist the complete dominance of Athens.

After the Persian occupation of Athens and the destruction of her city wall during the Persian invasion, Sparta had actually urged Athens to remain unwalled—a kind of arms control regime in which both states would forgo maximal self-defense in the name of retaining relative parity through mutual vulnerability.

Instead, Athens dispatched Themistocles, the hero of Salamis, to Sparta so that, by his delay and duplicity, they might have opportunity secretly to rebuild their city wall. Themistocles then urged the Athenians to build the "long walls" from Athens all the way to her port at Pireaus, giving her almost invulnerable city walls and secure access to her port and fleet at all times (1.90–91). In short, rather than being willing to trade some degree of vulnerability for stability and order, Athens's single-minded pursuit of her own absolute security came to breed instability and fear.

Now Athens had achieved virtual invulnerability. Her city had elaborate defensive walls; her port was immune from attack; her capabilities for import and trade were secure from all disruption, and, if all else failed, she possessed the capacity she demonstrated at Salamis to evacuate the city. But again, her quest of security had the inevitable effect of threatening all other states.

This is a classic trap for a superpower. Because it can pursue its own vision of security without restraint and without the need to negotiate, it runs the risk of actions that, while sensible from within its own strategic frame, have the effect of creating its own enemies. They emerge from framing its strategic problem too narrowly and over too short a time frame. Actions that are taken only in light of their short-term strategic advantage and oblivious to their inevitable consequences in the behavior of other rational actors in the strategic environment are the result.

What issues, in our own strategic environment, might we reflect upon in light of this historical analogue? Clearly, NATO expansion bears many of the same marks as Athens's encroachment into Corinth's strategic backyard. Megara, Pegea, and the refugee-inhabitants of Naupactus were all former inhabitants and allies of Corinth and Sparta. All sought alliance with Athens to be more secure against continued friction with Corinth and Sparta.

From Athens's perspective, welcoming them into alliance could only seem an excellent idea. They were new voluntary allies, eager to affiliate with Athens and the Delian League; they gave Athens access to new markets, new areas of influence traditionally beyond her sphere. They gave Athens military basing privileges in areas where she had interests, but had not been historically present. And at the moment, neither Sparta nor Corinth had the means to resist effectively Athenian expansion. From the Athenian perspective, her new alliances and forward bases would give her military strength that, even if Corinth or Sparta should wish to resist, she would by then be invincible.

But it was precisely these moves that made Corinth the implacable enemy of Athens. They caused Corinth to begin the drumbeat of resistance that would, in time, bring Sparta out of her seclusion and into open conflict with Athens as the head of a great alliance.

It may, then, provide some perspective on NATO expansion if one thinks of Russia and perhaps other parts of the former Soviet Union as the analogues to Corinth and Sparta. Do we, like Athens, fail to think through the downstream strategic consequences of alliances and military encroachments on powers that, for the moment, are incapable of resisting? Should it really surprise us if they feel threatened by those moves? Should we be surprised that our assurances of purely benign intent and motivations for the common good ring less true in Moscow than they do in Washington? Do we think through the more remote, but not unforeseeable, consequence of moves that make strategic sense in the short range, but induce fears and anxieties that may come back to haunt us?

A similar case can be made regarding Athens's pursuit of invulnerability in the construction of its walls and the long walls to its port, the Pireaus. The rhetoric of invulnerability surrounding National Missile Defense makes an interesting parallel. Surely defensive capability, pursued beyond a certain point, is as strategically destabilizing as augmented offensive capability. Sparta well knew that an Athens that could not be attacked by land made it, in regard to a land power such as Sparta, virtually invulnerable—as did Pericles when open warfare broke out. Thus his counsel to the Athenians during the first, Archidamian, phase of the war to remain behind the walls and let Spartan armies exhaust themselves in strategically meaningless forays into the Attic countryside.

Since others saw Athens's walls as a threat, giving her an offensive capability to act with impunity, perhaps we should be less surprised that allies as well as former adversaries are not convinced of the purity of our National Missile Defense aspirations. Sparta's proposal that Athens remain unwalled was, for its time and place, a rough equivalent of the ABM treaty. Athens's insistence of maximal self-defense was much like our threat to abrogate the stability of mutual vulnerability in the name of unilateral maximal self-defense. It is not difficult to foresee that National Missile Defense may well prove to be equally destabilizing and equally likely to precipitate arms races and organized resistance. One might also note the strategic irrationality of devoting large resources to preventing small numbers of missile attacks when covert delivery of the same weapons by Ryder truck remains a perfectly good alternative.

In the ancient world, as in ours, stability is achieved only at two points of the spectrum: where rough parity prevails and where absolute unilateral dominance is achieved on the model of the Roman Empire. The intermediate position of one rapidly advancing state in the presence of other states not yet peer competitors, but possessing the resources to oppose that state if they perceive the need to do so, is the most dangerous to manage. In the event, Athens seems to have possessed the will, but not the capability, to achieve absolute dominance in her world. The United States however, appears to lack both the capability and the will to strive for it—leaving aside the question whether it would be justifiable and prudent to do so.

The commercial policies of Athens were another important means by which she alienated her allies and frightened her potential enemies. For example, in 449/448, Athens decreed that all allied states must close their mints and imposed Athenian weights, measures, and coins on the allies.[6] Similarly, in her Megarian Decree, Athens used withdrawal of access to her markets as a blunt instrument with which to bludgeon states that did not acquiesce in her political and military dominance. Although the details are sketchy, clearly Athens's use of her commercial preeminence in a way that led to the detriment of other states was a major cause of the growing resistance to her empire.[7]

Correspondingly, there is a growing perception in much of the world that the World Bank, the International Monetary Fund, and "free trade" as the United States perceives it are just an extension of imperial dominance. Athens's challenge, like ours, was to make sure that her own growing wealth through trade was a perceived benefit to other Greek states, and not merely an additional weapon in her imperial quest.

Athens exercised a similar arrogance in her legal relations with other members of the Delian League. Athens decreed that all legal disputes between Athens and her allies must be tried in Athenian courts. Not only did this give Athens an obvious advantage but, given the democratic composition of those courts, it was an offense to allied aristocracy that they must be answerable to the Athenian popular will, the demos, in legal matters.[8] Just as the United States wishes to assert unique exemption from the emerging international legal regime of the International Criminal Court, Athens wished to retain its exceptional position among supposedly equal states.

If these assessments are valid, then clear strategic thinking in such environments must give due weight to balance and must take seriously the importance of the ripple effects of unilateral actions on the stability of the overall international system. Athens's failure to do that instilled fear and reinvigorated an opposing alliance that otherwise would have remained quiescent or, given more sensitive Athenian stewardship, even have joined Athens in a stable and unified Greek world.[9]

Rather than insisting on unilateral security, US abrogation of stable international arrangements (such as the ABM treaty), and US exemption from the International Criminal Court and similar efforts at universal and stable international institutions, we should see how our strategic thought could be informed by Athens's example. If it were, we would turn more to enhancing stability and less to provocative unilateral actions justified from the narrow perspective of the quest of unique defensive and offensive capabilities.

Be Imperial without Being Imperialist

Athens found itself, almost by accident, as an imperial power.[10] The structure of its military, its economy's dependence on freedom of navigation and trade, and the defensive requirements created by a still dangerous Persian empire all made Athens's far-flung empire (by ancient standards) worldwide. The strategic question before it was not whether to head an empire, but how to head it.

In this respect also, the situation of Athens bears close resemblance to our own. For the contemporary United States, just as for Athens, "The ideas that there are discreet baskets called 'foreign affairs' and 'domestic affairs' is no longer the case, if indeed it ever was. Increasingly, there are spillover effects, whether what is at stake is drugs, immigration, trade, ideas or email. Terrorism can come to our shores. So, too, can missiles. Fortress America, even if it were desirable, is simply not doable."[11]

The strategic goal, therefore, is to be imperial without being imperialist, without risking "imperial overstretch," in Paul Kennedy's famous phrase[12]. What that means, of course, is that one must use the instruments of national power to help shape the environment and the conduct of the "international community" such that it conforms to national interests. It also means that one must do so in such a way that one does not create enemies by imperialist conduct, and one must use one's resources prudently, and not to exhaust them in futile overreach.

We have already seen the many ways in which Athens created her own enemies. But even this might not have been fatal, had she used her superior power prudently, defeating enemies when necessary, but also co-opting them for her strategic purposes. Even having mismanaged the peace and empire handed her, Athens might still have been victorious strategically had she not overplayed her hand in foolish and strategically ill-advised military adventurism.

The most notorious example of this was the decision to dispatch her fleet for an assault on Sicily. Using the pretense of assisting the Attic population of Sicily, and attempting to counter a very distant threat of Syracuse, the principal city of the island, Athens moved to "order all ... matters in Sicily as ... best for the interests of Athens" (6.8.2). From a strategic perspective, such control of Sicily would have given Athens a second reliable source for importation of grain (which she was already importing on a commercial basis alone), a foothold in the western Mediterranean, and an anchor for her westward imperial expansion, bracketing the Peloponnesian alliance.

It fell to Nicias, the "Cassandra"[13] of Athenian strategy, to point out the foolishness of "grasping at another empire before we have secured the one we already have" (6.10.5). He alone grasped the problem with the enterprise being proposed: "[T]he Sicilians, even if conquered, are too far off and too numerous to be ruled without difficulty" (6.11.1). And Nicias alone proposed the most prudent strategic engagement with Sicily: "The Hellenes in Sicily would fear us most if we never went there at all, and next to this, if after displaying our power we went away again as soon as possible" (6.11.4).

But it was Alcibiades' speech that swayed the Athenian assembly. He said, "[W]e cannot fix the exact point at which our empire shall stop" (6.18.3), suggesting that even the conquest of Sicily could prove only the stepping-stone on the way to the conquest of Carthage as well.

In short, having gained a respite from war and having had yet another opportunity to negotiate from strength and to shape the international environment to Athens's liking, Athens chose instead a course of imperialist conquest that resulted in the utter destruction of her fleet and army. "When the news was brought to Athens, for a long while they disbelieved even the most respectable of the soldiers who had themselves escaped from the scene of action and clearly reported the matter, a destruction so complete not being thought credible" (8.1.1).

At every juncture, Athens overreached and failed to explore diplomatic arrangements that might have given her stability and an international environment to her liking. Although she had experienced strategic setbacks and defeats, at the time of the decision to go to Sicily Athens was very much in a position of strength, and had the opportunity to exploit her strategic advantage. Instead, she again sought military conquest far afield, making joint resistance to her efforts the only course of action available to her opponents. Finally, the combined forces of Syracuse and the Peloponnesian alliance crushed the Athenian forces in Sicily.

Although the conflict recommenced and continued, Athens' great strategic moment had passed. In every important sense, Athens had defeated herself. Her repeated and stubborn failure to grasp and manage her strategic environment effectively not only bred enemies; it finally squandered her military power itself.

What are the salient analogues between Athens's experience and our own? When this introduction was first written, it stated: "Obviously, the United States is not likely to send a large fraction of its military off in ill-conceived invasions of distant lands. But this particular course of action of Athens was, I would argue, merely a symptom of a deeper failure of strategic thought that does, indeed, bear important parallels to our situation." Now that a very large fraction of the U.S. military is apparently going to be in Iraq for a long time, the parallel is unfortunately, even more striking.

The fundamental strategic failure of Athens—and, indeed, of the entire Hellenic world—was the failure to grasp that the political structure of the polis, the sovereign city-state, was no longer adequate to the task of governance or of security in the international environment after the Persian War.

Although the Greek city-states had rallied effectively during that conflict in a military sense, they failed both during and after the war to build enduring political structures to match their military alliance. Athens did correctly perceive the need for a continuing military alliance in the face of the threat of Persia. But rather than building a truly effective "international" (i.e., interpolis) political organization, she converted the Delian League into her own fiefdom.

Had she instead found a way to use her unique power position to bring the economic, cultural, and political benefits of Athenian citizenship to her empire generally, she would have been spared the struggles of her tributaries to break free, and might have gained over time the voluntary affiliation of many of the members of Sparta's alliance as well. She might truly have been in her world the "city set on a hill" and the "light unto the nations" and have lived up to the role Pericles imagined for it: "[A]s a city, we are the school of Hellas" (2.41.1).

The United States, too, is at such a deciding moment. As sole remaining superpower, it too can elect to use that status to pursue and shore up narrowly conceived national interests. But there is no reason to expect the consequences of such behavior to be fundamentally different than those Athens experienced. While of course the degree of historical distance will make the details differ, the fundamental forces of human nature and statecraft are unchanged, and the consequences of a mode of behavior like that of Athens are foreseeable in any geopolitical time and place.

Alternatively, the United States might use this world-historical moment to help to forge the economic, diplomatic, and military structures that can genuinely serve the international common good. Surely Athens had that alternative. The worlds of trade her empire made possible might have continued to enrich the entire Greek world. Her experiments in democratic government, exported to some degree, might have been wedded with effective interpolis structures of government and law that would have stabilized the Greek world to the benefit of all.

Exactly what such structures should be for the United States and how they should be used is an issue of complexity and depth well beyond the scope of this introduction. But if the historical example of the Athenian empire is a useful conceptual model, these are the questions that should be at the center of strategic thought in the United States during this window of historical opportunity.

For example, the failure of Athens to imagine effective and just structures of law and governance larger than the city-state finally rendered her empire unmanageable and threatening to other powers. Had Athens used her political and military dominance as an opportunity to lead her world in the shaping of transnational (i.e., transpolis) governance structures, she might have led her world into a period of unprecedented peace and prosperity. Instead, as her power grew, she was less and less a leader of an alliance, and more and more dismissive of the legitimate claims and interests of her former allies.

In the contemporary context, the United States faces a world in which it is evident that any number of concerns and issues are no longer effectively addressed solely through the framework of state sovereignty. The United States says it bombs Kosovo in the name of universal principles, and in the same breath resists all efforts to institutionalize those principles in an international criminal court.[14]

Rather than funding and aggressively helping shape and reform the United Nations, the United States tends to give it inadequate resources and support and then complains of the UN's failures.

The United States complains that the Europeans are not bearing their fair share of costs for their own defense and that they lack the will and capability to respond to crises in Europe without United States assistance, but then it resists and threatens when they show evidence of organizing precisely such a capability.

These suggestions are, of course, merely schematic, and the issues are complex. But they do suffice to show ways in which the United States, like Athens, is deeply in love with the inherited international system (in their case, the polis; in ours, the sovereignty of the United States). Just like Athens, the United States finds it difficult to conceive larger international structures that would be fairer to all states and more effective in making its present favorable place in the world less a threat to other states.

It is difficult to say with precision, of course, what those structures should be. If the example of Athens does illuminate the present, it demonstrates that failure to make the conceptual leap when it is in one's power to do so safely can result in policies that are favorable to oneself in the short run, but that such a failure of foresight and imagination has inevitable and foreseeable negative consequences just over the horizon.

Like Athens, the United States finds itself at a moment history hands to few states, and then for only a limited period of time. It is a world-historical moment at which active engagement might well result in a permanent change to the geopolitical landscape of the world. In this book, I will explore the moral directions I believe these challenges will point us toward and the revisions in our thinking about the nature and role of the profession of arms these challenges will entail for the United States and its military.

Part One:
Moral Facets of Military Service

One

The Moral Framework of War

Violent conflict among human beings is, unfortunately, one of the great constants in our history as a species. As far back as we can see, the human species has engaged in war and other forms of organized violence. But it is equally true that, as far back as humanity has left written records, people have thought about morality and ethics. Although cultures vary widely in how they interpret death and killing from a moral and religious perspective, every human culture has recognized that taking human life is a morally grave matter; every human culture has felt the need to justify in moral and religious terms any taking of human life.

In the modern world, a large body of ethical and legal thought attempts to limit, constrain, and to establish criteria that sanction the use of violence in the name of the state and society. Through the mechanisms of The Hague and the Geneva Conventions, the Charter of the United Nations, military manuals such as the United States Army's *Law of Land Warfare*, and similar documents, modern governments and militaries attempt to distinguish "just war" and just conduct in war from other types of killing of human beings. Morally conscientious military personnel need to understand and frame their actions in moral terms so as to maintain moral integrity in the midst of the actions and stress of combat. They do so in order to explain to themselves and others how the killing of human beings they do is distinguishable from the criminal act of murder.

Attempts to conduct warfare within moral limits have met with mixed success. Many cultures and militaries fail to recognize these restraints, or do so in name only. The realities of combat, even for the best trained and disciplined military forces, place severe strains on respect for those limits and sometimes cause military leaders to grow impatient with them in the midst of their need to "get the job done." Events like the massacre at My Lai in Vietnam show that even forces officially committed to just conduct in war are still capable of atrocities in combat—and are slow to discipline such violations.

Despite these limitations, the idea of just war is one to which the well-led and disciplined military forces of the world remain committed. The fact that the constraints of just war are routinely overridden is no more a proof of their falsity and irrelevance than the existence of immoral behavior "refutes" standards of morality: we know the standard, and we also know human beings fall short of that standard with depressing regularity. The fact of moral failure, rather than proving the falsity of morality, points instead to the source of our disappointment in such failures: our abiding knowledge of the morally right.

Because of the importance of just war thinking, the general history, key provisions, and moral underpinnings of just war are things that every military person, and especially every senior leader, must understand and be able to communicate to subordinates and the public. It is important that senior leaders understand just war more deeply and see that the positive laws of war emerge from a long moral tradition that rests on fundamental moral principles. This chapter will provide that history, background, and moral context of ethics and war.

Background of Just War Theory

Most cultures of antiquity attempted to place some restraints on war. All recognized that there are some causes of war that are justifiable and others that are not. All recognized that some persons are legitimate objects of attack in war and others are not. All recognized that there were times, seasons, and religious festivals, and so on, during which warfare would be morally wrong or religiously inappropriate.

The roots of modern international law come from one specific strand of thought that emerged after the conversion to Christianity of the Emperor Constantine in the year AD 312. Although there were important ideas of restraint in war in pre-Christian Greek and Roman thought and, indeed, in cultures all over the world, it was the blend of Christian and Greco-Roman thought that led to the development of full-blown just war thinking over the following centuries.

Christianity before this time had been suspicious of entanglement in the affairs of the empire. For the first several centuries of the movement, Christians interpreted the teaching of Jesus in the Sermon on the Mount and other places quite literally, and saw themselves as committed to pacifism (the refusal to use force or violence in all circumstances). Although many appreciated the relative peace, prosperity, and ease of travel the empire's military force made possible, Christians felt prayer on behalf of the emperor was the proper limit of their support for it.

Much changed with Constantine. For many, war fought on behalf of a "Christian empire" was a very different thing than war on behalf of a pagan one. Furthermore, during the century following Constantine's conversion, the empire began to experience wave after wave of invasion from the north, culminating in the fall of the city of Rome itself in AD 410—a mere hundred years after Constantine.

It was in that context that Christian thinkers, most notably St. Augustine, a doctor of the church and bishop of Hippo in North Africa, first worked out the foundations of Christian just war thought. History, Augustine argued, is morally ambiguous. Human beings hope for pure justice and absolute righteousness. Augustine firmly believed that the faithful will experience such purity only at the end of time when God's kingdom comes. But until that happens, we will experience only justice of a sort, righteousness of a sort.

What passes for justice will require force and coercion, since there will always be people who strive to take more than their share, to harm others and to steal from them. In that world, the peacemakers who are blessed are those who use force appropriately to keep as much order and peace as possible under these conditions. The military officer is that peacemaker. Out of genuine care and concern with the weak and helpless, the soldier shoulders the burden of fighting to maintain an order and system of justice that, while falling far short of the deepest hopes of human beings, keeps the world from sliding into complete anarchy and chaos. It is a sad necessity imposed upon the soldier by an aggressor. It inevitably is tinged with guilt and mournfulness. The conscientious soldier longs for a world where conflict is unnecessary, but sees that the order of well-ordered states must be defended.

For Augustine and the tradition that develops after him, the theory of just war is an attempt to balance two competing moral principles. It attempts to maintain the Christian concern with non-violence and to honor the principle that taking human life is a grave moral evil. But it attempts to balance that concern with the recognition that, the world being what it is, the protection of innocent human life requires the willingness to use force and violence.

As it wends its way through history, the tradition of just war thought becomes more precise and more elaborate. In its development, it faces new challenges and makes new accommodations.

The Spanish in the New World, for example, were challenged to rethink the tradition as they encountered and warred against indigenous populations. Are such wars, too, governed by moral principles? Are all things permitted against such people? Or, it was seriously debated, are they even people, as opposed to some new kind of animal? Through that discussion came an expansion of the scope of just war principles to populations that did not share common cultures.

After the Protestant Reformation, as wars raged throughout Europe in the attempt to restore religious unity to Christendom, some thinkers (most notably Hugo Grotius) argued that just war must be severed from a distinctively Christian religious foundation. Human reason instead must provide a system for the restraint of war that would be valid despite religious difference, valid *etsi deus non daretur*, even if God did not exist! In other words, for Grotius and others, human reason is something shared by all people, regardless of their religion, ethnicity, or culture. Rationality, rather than revealed religion or religious authority, could suffice to ground moral thinking about war.

As a result of that secularization of just war thinking in Europe, the foundation was laid for the universal international law of the present international system. Natural law (moral rules believed to be known by reason alone, apart from particular religious ideas and

institutions) and the *jus gentium*, the "law of peoples"—those customary practices that are widely shared across cultures—would
ground just war in this changed religious-political system. In current international law, these accepted practices are called "customary international law," and they set the standard of practices of
"civilized nations."

Since virtually all modern states have committed themselves by
treaty and by membership in the United Nations to the principles
of international law, in one sense there is no question of their universal applicability. But the fact that the tradition has roots in the
West and in the Christian tradition does raise important multicul-
tural questions about it.

How does one deal with the important fact that Muslims have
their own ways of framing moral issues of war and conflict and even
of the national state itself that track imperfectly at best with the
just war framework? How does one factor in the idea of "Asian
values" that differ in their interpretation of the rights of individuals
and the meaning of the society and state from this supposedly universal framework? What weight should be given to the fact that
much of the world, while nominally consisting of nation-states on
the model established by the Peace of Westphalia in 1648, is in reality better described as "tribes with flags"? How does one deal with
the fact that, in much of the world, membership in a particular
ethnic group is more an indicator of one's identity than the name of
the country on one's passport?

All of these questions are the subject of intense scholarly
debate. All have real-world applications when we think about the
roots of conflict around the modern world and attempt to think
about those conflicts in the ways many of the participants do. But
for our purposes, we will need to set them aside in favor of making
sure we understand the just war criteria as they frame US military
policy and the existing framework of international law.

This limitation of focus is required not only by limitations of
space, but also by legal reality. Whatever one might want to say
about the important cross-cultural issues posed above, it remains
true that the United States and its allies around the world are committed by treaty, policy, and moral commitment to conduct military
operations within the framework of the existing just war criteria.
That fact alone makes it important that strategic leaders possess a

good working knowledge of those criteria and some facility in using them to reason about war.

Ideally, however, strategic leaders would also have some grasp of the ongoing debate about cultural diversity and the understanding of war in fundamentally differing cultural contexts.

The Purposes of the Just War Framework

The principles commonly called "just war criteria" provide an organized schema for determining whether a particular conflict is morally justified. As one might imagine, any such framework will inevitably fall short of providing moral certainty. When applied to the real world in all its complexity, inevitably persons of intelligence and good will can, and do, disagree whether those criteria are met in a given case.

Furthermore, some governments and leaders lie. No matter how heinous their deeds, they will strive to cast their actions in just war terms to provide at least the appearance of justification for what they do. If hypocrisy is the tribute that vice pays to virtue, it is testimony to the moral weight of the just war principles that just war language provides the shape of the lies even the greatest war criminals must tell. Rare indeed is the aggressor or tyrant willing to declare forthrightly the real causes and motives of his or her actions.

The twin realities of real-world complexity and the prevalence of lying about these matters suggest the importance not only of *knowing* the just war criteria as a kind of list, but also of skillful and careful reasoning using the just war framework as a strategic leader competency. Only if a leader is capable of careful and judicious application of just war thinking can he or she distinguish valid application of just war thinking from specious and self-serving attempts to cloak unjust action in its terms.

The Just War Framework

Moral judgments about war fall into two discrete areas: the reasons for going to war in first place and the way the war is conducted. The first is traditionally called *jus ad bellum*, or justice of going to war, and the second *jus in bello*, or law during war. Some interesting features of this two-part division are that different agents are primarily responsible for each and that they are to a large degree logically independent of each other.

Judgments about going to war are, in the American context, made by the National Command Authority and the Congress. Except at the highest levels where military officers advise those decision-makers, military leaders are not involved in those discussions and bear no moral responsibility for the decisions that result. Still, military personnel and ordinary citizens can and do judge the reasons given for entering into military conflict by those decision-makers and make their own determinations whether the reasons given make sense or not. A morally interesting but difficult question arises concerning one's obligations and responsibilities when one is convinced that recourse to war is not justified in a particular case.

Just conduct in war concerns the rules of engagement, choice of weapons and targets, treatment of civilian populations and prisoners of war, and so forth. These concern the "nuts and bolts" of how the war is actually conducted. Here the primary responsibility shifts from the civilian policymakers to the military leadership at all levels. Of course, political leaders and ordinary citizens have an interest in and make judgments about how their troops conduct themselves in war. Militaries conduct themselves in light of national values, and must be seen as behaving in war in ways citizens at home can accept morally.

Modern war, usually fought in plain sight of CNN and other media, is, for good or for ill, especially subject to immediate scrutiny. Political leaders and ordinary citizens react to virtually every event and require of their leaders explanations of why they conduct war as they do. That is another reason strategic leaders must be adept in explaining clearly and honestly the conduct of their forces within the framework of the just war criteria.

I turn now to a discussion of the particular criteria of just war. These are the tests one uses to determine the justification of recourse to war in particular circumstances.

We begin with the criteria for judging a war just in terms of going to war in the first place. Lists of these criteria vary somewhat in detail, but the following list captures the essential elements:

1. just cause
2. legitimate authority
3. public declaration
4. just intent
5. proportionality
6. last resort
7. reasonable hope of success
8. end of peace

The fundamental moral impulse behind just war thinking is a strong sense of the moral evils involved in taking human life. Consequently, the *ad bellum* tests of just war are meant to prevent too easy a recourse to force and violence to resolve conflict. Each of the tests is meant to impose a restraint on the decision to go to war.

The *just cause* requirement is that we have a legitimate and morally weighty reason to go to war. At one time, causes like "offended honor" or religious difference were considered good reasons for war. As it has developed, just war tradition and international law have restricted greatly the kinds of reasons deemed acceptable for entering into military conflict. The baseline standard in modern just war thinking is *aggression*. States are justified in going to war to respond to aggression received. Classically, this means borders have been crossed in force. Such direct attacks on the territorial integrity and political sovereignty of an internationally recognized state provide the clear case of just cause, recognized in just war theory and in international law (for example, in the Charter of the United Nations).

Of course, there are a number of justifications for war that do not fit this classic model. Humanitarian interventions, preemptive strikes, and assistance to a wronged party in another state's civil war, just to name some examples, can in some circumstances also justify use of military force, even though they do not fit the classic model of response to aggression. But the farther one departs from the baseline model of response to aggression, the more difficult and confusing the arguments become.

For that reason, international law and ethics give an especially hard look at claims of just cause other than response to aggression. To do otherwise risks opening the door for states to interfere at will with one another's territory and sovereignty.

The *legitimate authority* requirement restricts the number of agents who may authorize use of force. In the Middle Ages, for example, local lords and their private armies would engage in warfare without consulting with, let alone receiving authorization from, the national sovereign.

Nowadays, different countries will vary in their internal political structure and assign legitimate authority for issues of war and peace to different functionaries and groups. In the American context, there is the unresolved tension between the role of the president as commander in chief and the authority of Congress to declare war. The present War Powers Act (viewed by all presidents since it was enacted as unconstitutional, but not yet subjected to judicial review) has still not clarified that issue. But while one can invent a scenario where this lack of clarity would raise serious problems, in the National Command Authority and the Congress have found pragmatic solutions in every deployment of American forces so far.

The *public declaration* requirement has both a moral purpose and (in the American context) a legal one. The legal one refers to the issue we were just discussing: the role of Congress in declaring war. As we all know, few twentieth-century military conflicts in American history have been authorized by a formal congressional declaration of war. While this is an important and unresolved constitutional issue for the United States, it is not the moral point of the requirement.

The moral point involved is perhaps better captured as a requirement for delivery of an ultimatum before initiation of hostilities. Recall that the moral concern of just war is to make recourse to armed conflict as infrequent as possible. The requirement of a declaration or ultimatum gives a potential adversary formal notice that the issue at hand is judged serious enough to warrant the use of military force and that the nation is prepared to use that force unless the issue is immediately resolved.

The *just intent* requirement serves to keep the war aims limited and within the context of the just cause rationale for the war. Every conflict is subject to "mission creep." Once hostilities commence, there is always the temptation to forget what cause warranted the use of force and to press on to achieve other purposes—purposes that, had they been offered as justifications for the use of force prior to the conflict, would have clearly been seen as unjustifiable. The just intent requirement limits war aims by keeping the mind focused on the purpose of the war. Although there are justifiable exceptions, the general rule is that the purpose of war is to restore the *status quo ante bellum*, the state of affairs that existed before the violation that provided the war's just cause.

The *proportionality* requirement is that the damage done in the war should be worth it. That is to say, even if one has a just cause, going to war might be so costly in lives and property damage that it would be better to accept the loss. In practice, of course, this is a hard criterion to apply. Leaders and nations are notoriously inaccurate at predicting the costs of conflict as things snowball out of control.

But here, too, the moral point of just war criteria is to restrain war. And one important implication of that requirement is the demand for a good-faith and well-informed estimate of the costs and feasibility of redressing grievances through the use of military force.

The requirement that war be the *ultima ratio*, the *last resort*, also stems from a desire to make sure that force is used only reluctantly no matter how just the cause and no matter how well the other criteria may be met. The last-resort requirement acknowledges that the actual commencement of armed conflict crosses a decisive line. Diplomatic solutions to end conflicts, even if they are less than perfect, are to be preferred to military ones in most, if not all, cases. This is because the costs of armed conflict in terms of money and lives are so high and because armed conflict, once begun, is inherently unpredictable.

Judging that this criterion has been met is particularly difficult. Obviously, it cannot require that one has done every conceivable thing short of use of force: there is *always* more one could think to do. It has to mean doing everything that seems to a reasonable person promising. But reasonable people disagree about this. In the Gulf War, for example, many (including Colin Powell) argued that more time should have been given for sanctions and diplomacy to work.

The last requirement *ad bellum* is *reasonable hope of success.* Because use of force inevitably entails loss of human life, civilian and military, it is a morally grave decision to employ it. The reasonable hope criterion simply focuses thinking on the practical question: if you are going to do all that damage and cause death, are you likely to get what you want as a result? If you are not, if despite your best efforts it is unlikely that you will succeed in redressing the matter that brings you to war, then you are causing death and destruction to no purpose.

An interesting question is whether heroic but futile resistance is ever justified. Some have argued that the long-term welfare of a state or group may well require a memory of resistance and noble struggle, even in the face of overwhelming odds. Since the alternative is acquiescence to conquest and injustice, might it aid a group's long-term self-understanding to be able to look back and say, "At least we didn't die like sheep"?

The requirement of the "end of peace" requires us to ask whether the war in contemplation genuinely holds out the prospect of a "better peace" at its conclusion—a more stable and secure situation than that generating the present cause of war.

This completes the overview of the *jus ad bellum* requirements of just war. On the one hand, the categories and distinctions of the theory are not simple and clear. Neither individually nor together do they provide an algorithm that can generate for all fair-minded people a clear-cut and obvious judgment about a particular war.

On the other hand, it is important not to overemphasize the difficulty here. Although the language of just war is used by virtually all states and leaders in the attempt to justify their actions, not all uses of it are equally valid. Often it is not that difficult to identify uses that are inaccurate, dishonest, or self-serving. While there certainly are cases where individuals of good will and intelligence will disagree in their judgments, there are also many where the misuse is transparent.

Take, for example, Iraq's initial (and brief) attempt to justify its invasion of Kuwait on grounds that there had been a revolution in the Kuwaiti government and that the new legitimate government of Kuwait had requested Iraq's fraternal assistance in stabilizing the new government. Had this story been true, of course, Iraq would have been acting in conformity with international law and just war tradition by being in Kuwait. It is important to note that Iraq did apparently feel obliged to tell a tale like this, showing again the need of states to attempt to justify their actions in the court of world opinion in just war terms. Of course the story was so obviously false that within a matter of hours even Iraq stopped telling it. Indeed, few now even recall that it was told at the time.

The point in citing this example is to forestall an easy relativism. It is just intellectual laziness to conclude that, because these judgments are hard and people disagree about them in particular cases, the principles have no moral force or, worse, all uses of them are mere window dressing. In all moral matters, as Aristotle pointed out, it is a mark of an educated person not to expect more precision than the matter at hand permits. And in complex moral judgments of matters of international relations, one cannot expect more than thoughtful, well-informed, and good-faith judgments.

Jus in bello

We turn now to the *jus in bello* side of just war thinking. As I noted above, except at the highest levels of the military command structure, officers do not make the decision to commit forces to conflict. The moral weight of those judgments lies with the political leadership. But whether they are technically responsible for decisions to go to war or not, strategic military leaders will often be placed in the position of justifying military action to the press and the public.

The practical conduct of war *is*, however, the primary responsibility of military officers. They bear the responsibility for the training and discipline of military personnel. They issue the orders that determine what is attacked, and with what weapons and tactics. They set the tone for how civilians are treated and how POWs are captured, confined, and cared for. They determine how soldiers who violate order and the laws of war are disciplined and what examples are set for acceptable conduct in their commands.

Because of this weight of responsibility, officers at all levels must thoroughly incorporate thought about the *jus in bello* side of just war into standard operating procedure. It is an integral part of military planning, from the tactical issues of employing small units to the highest levels of grand strategy. US policy, national and universal values, and political prudence all require that officers plan and execute military operations with a clear understanding of just war requirements.

The major moral requirements of just war *in bello* boil down to two: discrimination and proportionality. Together, they set limits in the conduct of war—limits on *who* can be deliberately attacked and on *how* war can legitimately be conducted.

Although people often use the term *discrimination* almost wholly negatively (as in speaking of racial discrimination) the core meaning of the word is morally neutral. It refers to distinguishing between groups or people or things on the basis of some characteristic that distinguishes one group from another.

In the context of thought about war, the relevant characteristic upon which just war requires us to discriminate is *combatant status*. In any conflict, there are individuals who are combatants and others who are noncombatants. The central moral idea of just war is that only the combatants are legitimate objects of deliberate attack. By virtue of their "choosing" to be combatants they have made themselves objects of attack and have lost that immunity from deliberate attack all human beings have in normal life, and which civilians retain even in wartime. I put "choosing" in quotes, of course, because we all know that soldiers become soldiers in lots of ways, many of which are highly coercive. But they are at least voluntary in this sense: they did not run away. They allow themselves to be in harm's way as combatants.

Of course, in modern war there are lots of cases that straddle combatant and noncombatant status. The definition of the war conventions is straightforward: combatants wear a fixed, distinct sign of their status that is visible at a distance, and carry arms openly. But in guerilla war, combatants go to great lengths to blend in with the civilian population. In such a war, discrimination poses practical and moral problems.

When contractors are present on a battlefield or there is combat in urban environments and fighters (whether uniformed or not) are mixed in with civilian populations and property, discrimination between combatants and noncombatants is challenging both morally and practically.

It is less critical to focus on the hard cases than on the central moral point. War can only be conducted justly insofar as a sustained and good-faith commitment is made to discriminate between combatants and noncombatants and to deliberately target only the combatants.

Of course civilians die in war. And sometimes those deaths are the unavoidable by-product of even the most careful and conscientious planning and execution of military operations. Intelligence may be mistaken and identify as a military target a facility that turns out to be occupied by civilians or dedicated only to civilian use. Weapons and guidance systems may malfunction; causing weapons to land where they were not intended.

Just war theory recognizes these realities. It has long used the "principle of double effect" to sort through the morality of such events and justifies those which, no matter how terrible, do not result from *deliberate* attacks on civilians. Such accidents in the context of an overall discriminate campaign conducted with weapons that are not inherently indiscriminate are acceptable as "collateral damage."

What is *not* acceptable in just war thinking is the deliberate targeting of civilians or their use as "human shields." In practice, this means choosing weapons, tactics, and plans that minimize harm to innocent civilian populations, even if such choice places soldiers at (acceptably) greater risk.

The other major requirement of *jus in bello* is *proportionality*. It attempts to place limits on war by the apparently commonsense requirement that attacks be proportionate to the military value of the target. Judgments about these matters are highly contextual and depend on many dimensions of practical military reality. A massive bombardment of a town, for example, would be disproportionate if the military object of the attack is a single sniper. Proportionality is a requirement of the *jus ad bellum* tests as well, of course. There it requires a global assessment of the entire conflict. Here it is focused on individual tactical decisions regarding targets and weapons.

It is true, of course, that all sides violated these rules in World War II, especially in the uses of airpower. But the development of precision munitions and platforms for their delivery have, since that conflict, allowed the US military to return to greater compliance with the laws of war, even in air war. The moral need to do so that was part of the reason for those developments; but so, of course, was the fact that munitions that hit what they are aimed at with consistency and regularity are more militarily effective.

Contemporary Challenges to the Westphalian Model of Just War

Recent history has put considerable pressure on the under-standing of just war described above. From World War II on, a growing body of human rights and humanitarian law has evolved that, at least on paper, restrains the sovereignty of states in the name of protecting the rights of individual citizens. The Genocide Convention, for example, sets limits to what states may do to their own citizens and creates the right (and perhaps the obligation) of states to intervene to protect the rights of individuals when their violation rises to an unacceptable degree (which, unfortunately, is somewhat vaguely specified).

The conflict in Kosovo was clearly an example of intervention by NATO into the internal affairs of Serbia (recall: Kosovo was an integral part of Serbia in the policy of all the states involved). Very little of the national interest of the NATO powers, narrowly con-ceived, was involved in Kosovo. Humanitarian causes and human rights were cited to "trump" Serbian sovereignty. The action itself was not authorized by any resolution of the UN Security Council, to a large degree because the Chinese and the Russians feared the "porous sovereignty" precedent it would set.

Conversely, the failure to intervene in Rwanda was widely cited as a case where humanitarian concerns ought to have overridden sovereignty and national interest questions.

These examples point to a large and unresolved issue in contem-porary international ethics and law: the harmonization of state sover-eignty with issues of human rights and humanitarian intervention.

Another, even deeper, challenge is posed by the global "war" on terrorism. The term "war" is in quotation marks, because in many respects the nature of the conflict with al Qaeda and similar terror-ist groups of global reach departs markedly from the model of war between Westphalian sovereign states. Most obviously, terrorist groups are not state actors, so many of the conventions governing conflict between states apply imperfectly at best.

Unless terrorist groups are operating in international waters or in space, they do necessarily exist in some relationship to states. Some states deliberately and consciously sponsor and encourage them; others harbor them unknowingly; still others would like nothing better than to be rid of them, but have weak governments without the capability to dislodge them.

The Westphalian paradigm can be extended to cover the states that deliberately harbor them. The existence of a threat within the border of such states does constitute a just cause of war between the United States and its allies and the harboring state. One way of construing the conflict in Afghanistan is precisely this: that the Taliban government wished to shelter and protect al Qaeda on its territory and, after sufficient warning, placed its own continued existence in jeopardy.

The formalities of the current international system could be maintained with states that lack the power to dislodge terrorist groups, if they can be persuaded to request assistance from the United States or other powers to dislodge them, even if that "persuasion" results from considerable pressure.

But other possibilities present themselves. On one interpretation of the Bush administration's national security strategy, the nature of the terrorist threat warrants abandoning the "just cause" restriction to aggression received and adopting instead a more aggressive "preemptive" (or, perhaps better, "preventative") use of military force. This US policy might take one of two forms. In the first form, it might be a simple assertion of US military supremacy and lead to a fundamental recasting of the Westphalian assumption of the equality of sovereign states.

In the second form, the nature of the threat would lead to a reformulation of a common understanding of "terrorism" among the major powers. There might be a multilateral agreement, implicit or explicit, that some threats warrant interventions that might not pass the inherited "just war" tests of recent centuries. In that respect, just war would be returning to its origins: rather than seeing war as a conflict among sovereign states in response to aggression, the international community might see itself once again as defending a "tranquility of order" in the international system against incursions of alien systems and ideologies whose sole purpose is a disruption and displacement of that order. In other words, the globalized civilization grounded in democracy, human rights, free trade, communication, technology and science may be defending its civilization itself against forces that seek its complete destruction.

These aspects of the contemporary scene more than any others point to the need to think about just war in deeper historical terms. Existing international law has been formed almost entirely in accordance with the model of the Westphalian system, but if the second form of the global war on terrorism has some validity, those shared assumptions of the past several centuries may have less and less relevance. The original concerns of defending the stability of a system of civilization against fundamental attack may be the better analogue to present circumstances.

Conclusion

The moral tradition of just war and its partial embodiment in the laws of war at any moment are part of an ongoing evolution. They represent a drive to make practical restraints on war that honor the moral claim of individuals not to be unjustly attacked; at the same time, they recognize that use of military force in defense of individuals and values is sometimes a necessity.

All military officers charged with the grave moral responsibility of commanding and controlling military units and weapons must, if they are to conduct war morally, have a good working knowledge of the just war tradition and of the moral principles it strives to enshrine.

Above all, strategic leaders who set large-scale military policy, control training and organizational culture, and supervise the preparation of operational plans for national militaries need to think in ways deeply conditioned by just war principles. Because the weapons and personnel under their control are capable of causing such destruction, they, above all, must ensure that those forces act responsibly.

No amount of knowledge of the terms and concepts of just war will make morally complex decisions miraculously clear. But clear understanding of the concepts of just war theory and of the moral principles that underlie them help one analyze those choices. And in the rapidly changing international scene characterized by American military supremacy and non-state-actor attack, it may be that we are engaged in a rare, fundamental shift in the understanding of the international system such as we have not seen in four centuries.

If our military is to conduct itself in war in ways compatible with American national values, and if individual soldiers and officers are to be able to see themselves and their activities as morally acceptable, they must be able to understand the moral structure of just conduct in war. And, it is imperative that they integrate that understanding into the routines of decision-making in military operations.

Since the Gulf War, the language and concerns of just war have been integrated increasingly into the planning and execution of military operations. Military lawyers are fully integrated into modern targeting and operations planning cells of the US military. This is only an introduction to the terms and grammar of that thought. True facility in just war thinking only comes from careful and critical application of its categories to the complexities of real life and real military operations.

Two

Why Serve the State? Moral Foundations of Military Officership

Moral Talk and Military Virtue

In this chapter, I want to address what I think is the single most serious moral question any military officer needs to be clear about in her or his mind: the moral foundation of the enterprise of military service itself. Morally serious and thoughtful military officers feel a deep tension in the moral basis of their profession. On the one hand, there are very few places in our society where the concepts of duty and service above self have such currency. On the other hand, there is the reality that the military exists to serve the will of the political leadership of a particular state and will, at times, be employed for less-than-grand purposes.

Nobility, honor, and sacrifice are frequently invoked by military officers in ways that, for most of the rest of the society, might well sound quaint or outmoded. One hears talk about discipline and sacrifice of self for the good of others, but the military need not have a monopoly on such virtues. Even a pacifist such as William James sought some "moral equivalent of war" that could instill those values in civilian life![1]

There is, to some extent, cynicism in the military about this appeal to values and character. But as I said before, hypocrisy is the tribute that vice pays to virtue. Thus, the philosopher Michael Walzer observes that even if what political leaders say are lies, the fact that they feel *obligated to tell lies*, and more importantly *to tell those particular lies*, is probably a testament of the importance to all of us of the values their rhetoric expresses.[2]

Cynicism, then, is grounded in aspiration and to a great degree what drives cynicism is *disappointed* love. It seems to me that most of the young people who come to the military are full of the highest ideals. They are often disappointed to find that reality falls short of those ideals. To some degree, this is just frustration with the inherent limitations of human institutions. Disappointment upon the discovery of those limitations is a perennial characteristic of young people in all areas of life—and one to be cherished. It is the idealism of each new generation that gives us hope and that makes human progress possible. Of course, some of the frustration also flows from the failure of the bureaucratic system to implement effectively those values in institutional form. In any case it is important to acknowledge the deep longing for the values that underlies the disappointments rather than to focus on the cynicism.

The point is simple: the rhetoric of a strong moral basis of the military profession should be taken as a testimony to real and powerful aspirations—and aspirations to be deeply valued in the society. The value of those aspirations remains and should be honored, however far short of them we sometimes fall in experience. These aspirations are the foundation of the military virtues that preserve and sustain some of the noblest of human values: to serve others even at the cost of personal sacrifice, and to discipline one's mind and body so that it serves a purpose larger than self and the pursuit of pleasure.

Having said all that, however, it is important to note that there is a tension between these highest ideals of the military profession and another important reality of the military system. That other reality is that militaries exist as the servants of particular states and of their political leadership. If we believe Baron von Clausewitz that "War. . . is an act of policy,"[3] the military exists not to serve grand and universal moral principles, but simply to sacrifice itself for the political ends of the state. To put it bluntly, on Clausewitz's account, the real purpose of military leadership is simply to serve the national interest, as that interest is defined by political leadership. Viewed in this perspective, all the rhetoric about the high moral purposes of military service constitutes a verbal smoke screen behind which lurks a very unpleasant truth. If this perspective were the final word, then the truth would be that it is *functional* to persuade individuals to think about service in such moral terms, but only to make it psychologically easier for them to evade the true reality that they and their organizations exist only to serve the tribal interests of their state. And since states, on Clausewitz's analysis, are engaged in a constant struggle to advance their interests and to diminish those of other states, there is little here to be seen as morally grand.

Of course, if we were to think about the military this way, we would probably disguise that reality by invocation of ideas of the "self-defense" of the state. But such talk is vague. We know the core meaning of "self-defense:" self-defense is when someone is attacking us personally or when we resist a border incursion to protect the lives of fellow citizens in peril. In that narrow sense, all but absolute pacifists grant there is a right to self-defense. But it requires considerable intellectual sleight of hand to extend the concept of self-defense to foreign interventions—whether humanitarian or imperial—and to balance-of-power wars. In short, only rarely do militaries—and perhaps especially the US military—fight in wars that are genuinely defensive of political sovereignty and territorial integrity. More typically our wars serve something considerably broader and vaguer than strict self-defense would imply—something expressed with claims to vital national interests or important national values.

So we are now prepared to focus the fundamental question: What is the moral basis of states themselves that justifies our fighting to advance their interests? Certainly, one might say, it is only human individuals who make moral claims on us—and the use of force and violence might be justified in the defense of such individuals. But apart from conflicts of this type, where individuals are really being threatened, why should anyone be willing to kill and die for the state—an entity that, after all, is a relatively artificial construct, built on its own morally dubious foundation of conquest, domination, and destruction of other cultures?

What States Are and Why We Value Them

Our question was posed most sharply by St. Augustine—arguably the most influential thinker in Western intellectual culture. He wrote at one of those few real crossroads of history, with the Roman Empire collapsing around him, and the new age of darkness about to descend on the Western world. In his great work *The City of God*, Augustine reflects on the ruins of the Roman Empire. Romans of the old school he says, had a ready explanation for the collapse of their civilization: the fall of Rome was the fault of the Christians. For centuries, they reasoned, Rome was secure in its political and military strength because it worshipped the civic gods of Rome. In return, those gods protected the empire and sustained its armies. Indeed, for the Romans, much of religion had a primarily practical and civic function, and from the beginning, Christians' appeal to universal and transcendent values that embraced all of humanity seemed politically dangerous and profoundly un-Roman. From this pagan Roman perspective, a century of Christian rule had undermined those civic virtues and hence undermined Roman character and the will to fight.

It was Augustine's task, as he saw it, to refute the pagan charge. And in the course of doing it, his work ranged widely across Roman history, political philosophy, and philosophy of history. Augustine's ideas became quite literally the intellectual foundation of the Western Christian church and of Western political philosophy for the next thousand years. His influence is by no means absent even today. His point of departure was to question Roman assumptions about the glorious character of the state itself. With *painstaking* and—to Roman audiences, anyway—*painful* detail, he recounts the legends of the founding of Rome. Were not the legendary founders of the state, Romulus and Remus, suckled by wolves? Was the state not founded on murder and treachery?

Then, in one of the most famous passages in the entire work, Augustine offers his own view of the glory that was Rome:

> Remove justice, and what are kingdoms but gangs of criminals on a large scale? What are criminal gangs but petty kingdoms? A gang is a group of men under the command of a leader, bound by a compact of association, in which plunder is

divided according to an agreed convention. If this villainy wins so many recruits from the ranks of the demoralized that it acquires territory, establishes a base, captures cities and subdues peoples, it then openly arrogates to itself the title of kingdom, which is conferred on it in the eyes of the world, not by the renouncing of aggression but by the attainment of impunity. For it was a witty and truthful rejoinder which was given by a captured pirate to Alexander the Great. The king asked the fellow, "What is your idea, in infesting the sea?" And the pirate answered . . . The same as yours, in infesting the earth! But because I do it with a tiny craft, I'm called a pirate: because you have a mighty navy, you're called an emperor."[4]

On Augustine's view, there simply is no moral difference between states and bands of pirates. There is only the difference of scale, which can make the state seem grand while the robber band is simply evil. Both depend for their success on a kind of internal harmony and organization (what we might call "military virtues"), and both measure success by their ability to take and destroy the lives and property of others.

In accordance with this analysis of the state, Augustine counsels Christians to look to their true home, not in the City of Man or the Earthly City, as he calls it, but in the City of God—a "city" of universal and transcendent value. Only in such a city can human beings find spiritual and moral rest: as he wrote in another work, "you have made us for yourself, and our heart is restless until it rests in you."[5]

But for the time being we live in both cities. In this life, and in this history, we must struggle amid the shades of gray of the state, of warfare, and of injustice, doing what we can to make things better and more peaceful than they would otherwise be, but not expecting purity. We are to live, then, "between the times"—aware of the City of God, but not trying "before its time"[6] to live as if we were its citizens exclusively.

It may be necessary to go to war in service of the *relatively good* state, which is all that stands between us and complete political and moral chaos—a chaos Augustine quite literally saw on the horizon as Rome fell and barbarian armies advanced on his own city in Africa. But such wars are to be entered "mournfully," free of false hopes of creating a City of God amid the shadows of the City of Man.

This Augustinian line of thinking laid the foundation for the classic Christian (and, later, secular international-legal), justification for participation in warfare: just (or justified) war theory. This theory worked out a place for moral conduct of soldiers intermediate between the pacifism of the early church and the amoralism of the nihilist's denial that moral categories apply to war at all.

Of course, this tradition has undergone enormous elaboration and qualification as it has wended its way through Western intellectual history—and through the changing political contexts in which it has been worked out. For most of that next thousand years after Augustine, the Western world was a backwater compared to the stronger and more sophisticated civilizations of the East, first of the Byzantine Empire, and then of the new Islamic civilization centered in Baghdad. But within the West, the ideal was a model of a unified Christian civilization, centered in Rome and under the authority of the bishop of Rome, the pope. On this understanding, wars were justified, at least theoretically, as responses to disruptions of the order of that civilization.

So it is important in our thinking about fighting in *defense of states* to remind ourselves that the state as we know it is a fairly modern invention. For much of history, and for many cultures, *the state as we think about it* did not exist at all, or its existence was highly relativized by other forms of human organization. As I indicated, in the West it was not until the period after the Reformation that the nation-state, with its claims to sovereignty and territorial integrity, became the dominant institution. Prior to that, European nations and political leaders were subordinate in principle, and often in fact, to the ideal of a universal Christendom. Similarly, to this day, the Islamic world affirms in principle the unity of all Muslim peoples and cherishes the ideal of gathering all these peoples into a single political order with a single political head. This Muslim civilization as a unified entity is set in contrast to the *dar al harb*, the world of conflict that lies outside the order of Islamic civilization. And in many parts of the postcolonial world—in Rwanda, Bosnia, and Ethiopia, to name only a few examples—we discover daily to our horror that the states on the map correspond poorly, if at all, with the boundaries of the tribes and clans to which the inhabitants belong.

The development of the concept of states with rights to territorial integrity and political sovereignty and of a world system that takes that form of organization as fundamental is an attempt to give a moral shape and definition to the realities of post-Reformation Europe. It became obvious as Europe exhausted itself in the religious wars following the Reformation that any ideas of a unified Christian empire were no longer tenable. In place of the earlier ideal, laws and customs of international relations evolved to deal with those new realities, and particularly to put an end to perennial war over religious differences. In 1648, the end of the Thirty Years War, the futility of restoring political and religious unity by force was finally accepted and, the European states crafted the Peace of Westphalia. In this new Westphalian international system, religion would no longer be a factor in determining alliances or granting or withholding citizenship. Nor would it be a cause of war. Instead, Europe was organized into nation states of differing religious systems. Here the rules of the game were that the internal matters of states were their own business. It is from this we get the modern international system, in which political sovereignty and the territorial integrity of those states are the highest values. The whole body of international law is founded on this idea of the sovereign state as an entity closely analogous to John Stuart Mill's idea of the free individual, able to do as he or she sees fit in matters that affect only individual welfare. And correlatively, each free individual is at liberty to pursue the life and beliefs that seem to him or her most likely to lead to happiness, free from the interference of others.

The whole body of Christian and medieval thought about the just war is transposed in this new environment into a secular version of the theory. Here *jus ad bellum*, the reasons for going to war, are increasingly defined in terms of the defense of the twin principles of the new international system: territorial integrity and the political sovereignty of states.

The military, too, came to have a rather different conceptual framework in this model of the international system than it had in medieval Europe or in the Islamic world. Naturally, I do not mean to defend the Crusades or the military aspects of the Islamic concept of jihad (religious struggle) to expand the realm of Islam. But it is important to note that those notions of military struggle place the activities of the warrior within a supposedly universal moral and religious framework—*in principle* the soldier fights not for the local interests of a particular ruler or state but in the name of values believed to be universal and transcendent.

With the rise of the nation-state, the role of the military is set in a much smaller, and probably more realistic, context: that of defending a particular political and social order in the face of threats to it by other militaries in the service of other individual states. It is an axiom of this new model of international order that all states *have equal moral claims* to territorial integrity and political sovereignty, and that *each state* has the right to be free of aggression by others and to use its military in defense of those rights. Although occasionally the rhetoric is more grandiose, perhaps especially in American political discourse (the "war to end all wars," "defending democracy" or civilization itself, or "defeating Communism"), the "official rules" of the international system were built on the idea of the fundamental equality and internal sovereignty of all states.

There is an implication in this for the morality of the military. In the Westphalian international system, military officers are moral equals, regardless of the state they serve. This is the modern European understanding of the moral foundation of officership— that all military officers are morally coequal members of the profession of arms. Even though they may be called upon by their political leadership to fight each other, and to fight in wars of unequal moral worth, this is not strictly an issue for the military professional. On this model, the moral demands on the military profession are great, but they are also delimited: the officer is obliged to serve the state with integrity and to conduct military operations in a professional manner, disciplining subordinates and ensuring that they conduct themselves within the bounds of the laws and customs of war. But it is *not* the moral responsibility of the officer to assess the moral worth of the state itself or, in all but the most extreme cases, the justice of the war the officer is ordered to conduct.

But in this Westphalian model, one may still ask our fundamental question: What is the moral basis on which officers of these particular states can justify killing and dying for their interests? Some states, after all, fall far short of being bearers of universal moral, religious, or political truth. The case for a moral basis of violence is a hard one to make, but it is important to make it. Let us look only at our own history. Suppose someone said that the United States is built on the morally very questionable foundation of conquest of the indigenous civilizations by disease and war, and of dishonorable and dishonest dealings with both Native American peoples and with Mexico. Or that its current territory is the product of complex forces and trends that rather arbitrarily interacted to make the United States have the borders it now has. Suppose that person went on to say that racism is alive and well in American life, and that the relations between the sexes are far from fair and equal. To that litany of charges, what can any well-informed and educated American say but "true"?

Admiral James Stockdale has written a fine essay in which he discusses his observations on education and the prisoner-of-war experience.[7] He points out the dangers of the POW with so little education or such a misguided understanding of patriotism that the realities of a less-than-perfect American society could be presented by an enemy and came as a revelation to the POW. His point, I think, is a profound one: if one is to serve the state as a thinking military officer, one must serve the state *as it is*, not the fantasy state of America's highest ideals and ambitions. In this regard, Augustine's somber estimate of the state—of any state—is far closer to reality than the "alabaster cities" whose gleam is "undimmed by human tears" of our best national song. The educated POW would understand that such a litany of injustice, with the appropriate regional variations, would be the story behind virtually every other state in the world, too.

I believe, however, that we are in a phase of human history in which this Westphalian state system and the model of military officership it generates are undergoing profound change. The change was symbolically marked by General Eisenhower's conduct at the end of World War II. When the German general von Arnim was captured, he requested a meeting with General Eisenhower—a request completely reasonable on the Westphalian model of the moral equality of members of the profession of arms. Eisenhower refused, however, saying,

The tradition that all professional soldiers are comrades in arms has ... persisted to this day. For me, World War II was far

too personal a thing to entertain such feelings. Daily as it pro-
gressed there grew within me the conviction that, as never
before. . . the forces that stood for human good and men's
rights were . . . confronted by a completely evil conspiracy with
which no compromise could be tolerated.[8]

The Changing Character of State Sovereignty: Implications for Military Officership

Clearly, General Eisenhower's attitude marks a change from the
idea of morally equal military professionals to one of military service
set once again in the framework of universal moral questions about
the nature of the states officers serve. And even in cases where that
model applied less clearly (Vietnam or the Korean War, for example), American political discourse has tended to follow that trend
in the post–World War II environment, speaking of each engagement as a battle of moral and human good against unalloyed
human evil. Of course, insofar as military power and deterrence
were *actually* (rather than simply *rhetorically*) in the service of the
resistance to Communism, those claims made considerable sense.
At the very least, it was true that the form Communist states took
were affronts to human dignity and liberty on a scale comparable to
that of the Nazis.

But as everyone now knows and no one fully understands, we
are now in a "post–cold war world" or "a new world order." There is
much that only time can tell us about what this means, but I wish
to note at least a few of the trends it implies, and then to return to
our central question: What is the moral foundation of military officership in this new order? Of course much of what I'm about to say
is common knowledge. Nevertheless, I think it important and necessary to rehearse these considerations.

The first and most dramatic change in our new environment is
that it is no longer bipolar, either conceptually or militarily. For the
majority of the post–World War II period—and the entire history of
the United States Air Force as a separate service branch, one might
note—the important military and political power in the world was
effectively divided into the two spheres of superpower influence.
But we do not yet know what will replace that system. Will it be a
monopolar world, with the United States dominating as sole

remaining superpower? While theoretically a possibility, I do not think such an option is likely to materialize. There are too many strong nonsuperpowers that have their own claims and agendas in this world, and the United States lacks the will and desire (fortunately, in my opinion) to impose on the world a Pax Americana by the same brutal means the Romans needed to impose the Pax Romana in Augustine's time.

If that is so, then we look forward to a much more complex and multipolar world than we have experienced in our recent history. We see this tension in all our recent military deployments, and it appears as a kind of national schizophrenia about the uses of military power, and therefore also of the moral foundations of military officership. Let me say, too, that while I have clear opinions about the prudence and desirability of both of the examples I am going to use, I do not plan to comment on those opinions here. Rather, I choose these examples as illustrations of what seems to be our confusion in thinking about the moral basis for the use of military power.

Take the Gulf War. No war since World War II has so clearly matched the Westphalian paradigm: Kuwait, a sovereign state, internationally recognized, has its territorial integrity and political sovereignty directly and unambiguously attacked. That state requests help from the international community to restore it among the nations of the world. States respond; aggression is rolled back; Kuwaiti sovereignty is restored. This is the classic Westphalian story with a happy ending.

But, say the critics, the moral basis of the Gulf War is tainted. Despite all the rhetoric of international law and multinational coalitions, so the argument goes, *really* the war was about oil and economics. The implication seems to be that *because* there were important international economic interests involved in that war, the presence of such interests makes the motives impure. "No blood for oil!" went the chant. But would "Blood for Kuwaiti sovereignty!"—in the absence of oil—spark the enthusiasm of the critics?

For the sake of contrast, let us briefly examine the Haiti deployment to restore the Aristide presidency. Here, in extreme contrast to the Gulf War, it is very hard to make a case for a crucial American interest. True, here there was a clear and unmistakable violation of human rights and of respect for law and international diplomacy, and there was real repression of the smallest stirrings of internal resistance. Yet here the criticism was the opposite to that of the Gulf War: the cry, I suppose, would be "No blood for the rights of foreigners when there is no national interest involved!"

These examples seem to me to point to the horns of the Westphalian dilemma in its post–cold war form: Is military power to be used in the service of national interests, wherever they are? If so, then claims to higher moral justifications are unnecessary and misguided! In other words, Clausewitz's word is the final word, and war really is just politics by other means.

Alternatively, is military power, freed from the fairly artificial and historically abnormal framework of the bipolar superpower world, now at last at liberty to serve the universal moral ends of promoting democracy, supporting human rights, and removing oppressors, to the cheers of the oppressed? If so, how and why should national political leaders be willing to spill the blood and spend the treasure of their individual nations in the service of the lives and rights of foreign nationals?

We are now deeply ambivalent about these alternatives, and much of our national confusion about the role of US foreign policy generally, and of the purposes of military power specifically, results from this conflicting pair of models for thinking about force projection. Only time will provide some of these answers, but let me sketch two models for the moral basis of officership in this changing environment.

The first accepts the Westphalian model of international organization, but with modification. Michael Walzer, in his fine book *Just and Unjust Wars*, attempts to work out why national loyalties should matter to people. His argument is that even though existing states and their boundaries result from arbitrary mapmaking and histories of conquest, reasonably good states can emerge, and the twin rights of territorial integrity and political sovereignty can create a "space" (both literal and metaphorical) where a group of people can attempt to work out a "common life." He explains this concept of common life as follows:

> Over a long period of time, shared experiences and cooperative activity of many different kinds shape a common life. "Contract" is a metaphor for a process of association and mutuality, the on-going character of which the state claims to pro-

tect against external encroachment. The protection extends not only to the lives and liberties of individuals but also to their shared life and liberty, the independent community they have made, for which individuals are sometimes sacrificed.[9]

On this model, therefore, one serves the state in order to protect that "common life" the officer shares with fellow citizens. One recognizes the complexity and often the moral ambiguity of the processes that give rise to that common life. But one recognizes as well that the persistence and flourishing of that common life is a condition for human welfare and goods less tangible than life and property—the goods of shared memory, common symbols, and history and culture. It provides a language to try to articulate why, in reasonably good states, it matters to be an American or a Haitian, over and above the good of individual survival.

The foundation of this idea of "common life" is Westphalian, and is applicable to every society possessed of sufficient historical continuity. It is here, I think, that General Eisenhower's perspective should play a part. If the moral basis of states is that they create and maintain the "space" within which a common life can flourish, it is obvious that states succeed in doing this to widely varying degrees. Walzer continues his argument:

> The moral standing of any particular state depends upon the reality of the common life it protects and the extent to which the sacrifices required by that protection are willingly accepted and thought worthwhile. If no common life exists, or if the state doesn't defend the common life that does exist, its own defense may have no moral justification.[10]

It is this reality that we encounter with ever greater frequency in the new world order—of "states" with borders on maps and seats of government that correspond poorly, if at all, to the common life (and often common *lives* of multiple communities) contained within their borders. When we survey the horrors of Bosnia and Somalia, to name only two examples, we see clearly states of this type—states that contain no clear common life, and states that fail to protect even the individual lives and rights of their inhabitants, let alone this grander concept of common life. These situations call to the sympathies of all of us, and cry out for "someone" to do something to remedy the situation. Yet it is here that the moral tug collides with the Westphalian reality: What individual states are willing to sacrifice their citizens' lives in such a cause?

It may prove to be utopian, but is it too farfetched to imagine that the new world order, premised not only on the collapse of a bipolar world but also on the growing world culture of communication and global awareness, may also work a change in the moral foundation of military officership? If Walzer is right, and states are worth defending for the common life they protect, may we not be witnessing the painful, but inevitable, birth of a truly global common life? As we watched the failure of international institutions to deal effectively with Somalia and Bosnia, were we perhaps feeling the clear indications of the inadequacy of existing international mechanisms to deal with the problems of states that do not protect a genuine common life? The United Nations was founded when there came to be a clear realization of the need for effective mechanisms for collective security; now, I think, we are entering a period when farsighted leadership would see the need for a military dedicated to the high moral purpose of defending fellow citizens of the global common life.

In a profound speech to a joint session of the United States Congress in 1994, South African president Nelson Mandela said the following:

> In an age such as this, when the fissures of the great oceans shall, in the face of human genius, be reduced to the narrowness of a forest path, much revision will have to be done of ideas that have seemed as stable as the rocks, including such concepts as sovereignty and the national interest....
>
> If what we say is true, that manifestly, the world is one stage and the actions of all its inhabitants part of the same drama, does it not then follow that each of us ... should begin to define the national interest to include the genuine happiness of others, however distant in time and space their domicile might be?[11]

Mandela's vision of the new world order has much to recommend it. To a large degree, it seems to reflect accurately the global convergence we daily witness around us. It reflects, too, the growing sense that the existing structures of international relations are increasingly inadequate to the tasks now facing them in the post–cold war world.

But it leaves much unresolved at the practical level. Are the armed forces and leaders of individual nation-states prepared to enlist in the service of such a vision? Can we ask the military of our state to fight and die in the name of such a global vision of our interests?

Clearly, it is too early to tell. But equally clearly, the moral foundation of military officership is showing all the signs of a fundamental revision. The world of the Peace of Westphalia is passing from the scene, and we only begin to glimpse what will take its place. Young officers enter a military full of challenges, different in kind from those that faced any of their predecessors. It is theirs to take the lead, not only in command, *but in thought*, about what that future will be.

Three

The Normative Dimensions of Military Professionalism

Much has been written in recent years about the state of professionalism in the contemporary officer corps in the United States. This chapter explores the concept of professionalism itself as a normative term. From an ethical perspective, the question is how to understand professionalism so that two equal values, somewhat in tension with one another, are preserved: the unquestioned subordination of military officers to constitutionally legitimate civilian leadership; and, the equally important role of the officer corps in providing professional military advice, unalloyed with extraneous political or cultural considerations.

A good deal of the contemporary confusion in the profession results from distorted understanding of these issues. Some emphasize subordination, to the virtual neglect of legitimate professional expertise; others emphasize professional expertise, to the point of threatening insubordination of the military to the political leadership. Proper conceptual clarification of the terms will substantially reduce those misunderstandings.

"Professionalism" as a Normative Term

Typical military officers have a fairly limited moral vocabulary. The central terms are "integrity" and "professionalism," and those

55

terms are rarely examined critically. One praises an officer by saying he or she has "integrity," and one criticizes by saying he or she lacks it. One criticizes a wide range of behaviors, from how an individual dresses to the orderliness of an office or the individual's ethical character by saying they show a lack of professionalism, and one praises an equally wide range of conduct by saying the individual "is a real professional."

A professional group can successfully manage to maintain a widely shared standard of conduct and professional self-understanding, even with such unexamined vocabulary, during times of relative stability in the profession and its environment. When members of the profession are engaged in common activities, when the environment and culture in which they do their professional work are stable, and when the assumptions about the nature and purpose of their work are widely shared, critical examination of that vocabulary is perhaps unnecessary.

But during times of great change in the nature, function, and security of the profession, such unexamined unanimity will be found inadequate to articulate the nature of the challenge. If, for example, a profession has become accustomed to acting in a given sphere with complete autonomy, great tensions will arise when societal or legal changes challenge or limit that autonomy. Consider, for example, the great tensions managed care has precipitated in the medical profession. Increasingly, medical professionals question whether physicians can be "true professionals" as their autonomy in medical practice is increasingly circumscribed by case managers and preferred-provider limitations. Was the way physicians experienced the conditions of their work before managed care a necessary condition of their professionalism? Or are the stresses now being experienced simply the kind of stress any change inevitably brings with it?

By any measure, the officer corps of the US military is moving through a period of enormous change in the nature, purpose, and meaning of the profession. In recent years, it has been deprived of its central defining threats—threats that have shaped the nature and practices of the military culture for several generations. It has experienced a wrenching reduction in the size of the force, which in turn has had enormous effects on the normal officer career progression and prospects for professional advancement. Its equipment is aging and, it increasingly appears, not highly relevant to the kinds of military engagements it is being asked to perform. Among the military services, the army in particular is undergoing a process of very rapid transformation in force structure, equipment, and doctrine that many do not fully understand or, in some cases, endorse.

Not surprisingly with so many shifts occurring, military officers in their professional role are somewhat unsure of themselves, a typical sign of a profession in transition and change. Its junior members (captains) are leaving the profession at higher rates than expected. Significant numbers of the most successful colonels are declining brigade command, thus effectively refusing professional advancement. Distrust between levels of the profession is extremely high, and morale is low.[1]

As is to be expected, the moral vocabulary of the profession is invoked to "explain" what is occurring among military officers. When officers do not behave in ways associated with earlier, more settled times, they are seen as "lacking integrity" and manifesting a diminished sense of "professionalism."[2] When they rank force protection as their primary mission in far-flung peacekeeping operations, they manifest already declining "professionalism." When they fail to embrace the profession as essential to their personal sense of identity and leave military service after short careers, those who remain are inclined to blame the departing individuals for their failure to share the "professional" ethos.

In fact, however, the departing individuals may be barometers indicating that the shifts in the role and mission of the profession have been so great as to change their relation to the profession dramatically. Further, they may reflect shifts in broader societal attitudes toward work, family, and career loyalty that merely play out in military culture in distinctive ways, but which have significant parallels throughout the society.[3]

Before too quickly deploying the standard vocabulary of professionalism, one should pause and inquire whether the vocabulary is indeed adequate to the task. Unless the central terms are conceptually precise, one runs the risk of invoking the military's standard limited moral vocabulary in criticism of individuals and classes of officers without accurately grasping the phenomenon one wishes to describe.

Eliot Friedson shrewdly raises a caution about too uncritical an embrace of the language of "professionalism" to exhort and criticize.

He notes the ideological sense of "profession" that allows the term to be used manipulatively: "The ideology may be used by political, managerial, and professional authorities to distract workers from their objective lack of control over their work, to lead them to do the work assigned to them as well as possible, and to commit them to means and ends others have chosen for them."[4]

Friedson is suggesting that in circumstances in which workers have lost control over their work or become disillusioned with the resources and support available to them, one would expect their superiors to employ the language of professionalism. The function of that language is to motivate workers to labor on, oblivious to the objective shifts in the character and meaning of their work. In such a circumstance, professional workers are no longer able to define the scope and nature of their core professional competencies, and are being tasked to accomplish missions for which they feel ill prepared by their professional experience.

Before embracing the conclusion that the root problem with the contemporary officer corps is a declining sense of professionalism, one should step back and determine the nature and purposes of the military officer corps as professionals. What is the fundamental nature and purpose of the profession? What are the timeless attributes of the profession that must be maintained in all circumstances, and what elements are contingent on particular historical and political circumstances? Are there elements that have historically been foundations of the self-understanding of the profession that are in flux?

Necessarily, one cannot address the issue of military professionalism ahistorically. Besides the obvious changes in the size and mission and the generational shifts in attitudes among younger officers, there are still larger shifts in the society from which the military recruits and within which it functions. Is the "postmodern" military a reality?[5] Certainly the internal and external environments within which the military functions are changing dramatically. Charles Moskos suggests eleven critical dimensions in which the military of the future will be fundamentally different from the military of the cold war—dimensions as diverse as the military's media relations, force structure, perceived threat, and the roles of women and spouses in military culture.

If such fundamental changes are, indeed, in progress, it seems unlikely that the professional ethos of the military will remain constant. Clearly, in a time of enormous change in the nature, scope, purpose, and size of the military, some confusion and reconsideration of purpose are inescapable and appropriate. In this chapter, we will examine the question of the nature of the military as a profession in the contemporary context. Some reflections on continuity and change of the professional military ethic as it emerges from this period of transition and uncertainty will be offered. And we will consider some normative suggestions regarding the shape military professionalism should take as the dust settles and the US military emerges from this time of transition and uncertainty.

The Military Profession in a System of Professions

A useful conceptual framework for thinking about professions is provided by Andrew Abbott's book *The System of Professions. An Essay on the Division of Expert Labor.*[6] Fundamental to Abbott's conception of professions is the idea that professions apply bodies of abstract knowledge to a sphere of professional tasks. Societal recognition of the appropriateness of a profession's sphere constitutes its professional "legitimacy." Perhaps most important to Abbott's view is the idea that legitimacy is not a fixed, immutable fact. Rather, professions jockey for position within a given society as different professions and nonprofessional groups attempt to gain jurisdiction over spheres of human labor that previously have belonged to other professional groups, or, alternatively, as professions attempt to protect their historical jurisdiction from encroachments by competitor professions.

One may ask whether the current uncertainty in the military officer corps is a manifestation of precisely this kind of jurisdictional conflict in progress. If the answer is affirmative, then the changed character of the geopolitical situation (an "external system change" in Abbott's vocabulary) has required the military services to engage in a wide range of activities that differ from the classic cold war war-fighting mission. Those new demands and tasks differ considerably from the activities, behaviors, and expectations that defined the profession for the previous fifty years.

The jurisdiction of the US Army throughout the cold war, for example, was large-scale armored and combined arms land warfare. While it could be assigned many other tasks, the core jurisdiction has remained fixed, and the culture, values, and professional standards of the current army remain linked to that core jurisdictional function. Individuals raised in that professional culture may well experience professional confusion and uncertainty in the face of new and different tasks. Much of their professional self-understanding has been bound to those tasks, and much of their body of professional knowledge, expertise, and agreed-upon ways of functioning is tied to that context.

It is to be expected that, in the face of quite different expectations, they question whether the new demands are consistent with their understanding of the profession. If this is the correct view of what is occurring,[7] then the question before the profession (in terms of Abbott's framework) is whether to compete in a jurisdictional competition for new roles and missions, or to cede the territory to other professional contenders. In other words, given that political leadership and American society generally are choosing to engage in peacekeeping and peace-enforcing missions around the globe, the army must either adapt to them or prepare for considerable professional stress.

The army is analogous to a species that may or may not successfully adapt to a changing environment. In Abbott's view, professions live and die in the face of the evolutionary pressure of adaptation. Those that cling to forms superseded by external change face the prospect of joining astrologers and phrenologists in the dustbin of cultural history.

One common view—perhaps the majority view within the profession—takes for granted the idea that the army can and must embrace all tasks assigned by "society," and views the reluctance to do so on the part of some officers as evidence of a declining sense of professionalism in the officer corps. As Don Snider, John Nagl, and Tony Pfaff state the matter:

> In a democracy, an Army does not get to choose the missions it accepts—at least, no professional army does. The hesitancy of the United States Army to accept wholeheartedly the missions it is currently being given strikes the authors of this

paper as cause for concern in the context of military professionalism. We believe that means defining the Army's organizational purpose, its essence, simply as serving the American society, and fighting the conflicts they approve, when they approve them. Any other essence or purpose statement places the institution in the illegitimate and unprofessional position of declaring its intellectual independence from the society it was formed to serve.[8]

A number of points are striking about this analysis. First, it asserts that "intellectual independence from the society" is, per se, unprofessional. Second, it presupposes that the "hesitancy" of the army to accept current missions is itself "cause for concern" regarding the Army's professionalism. Third, it offers a definition of the core professional function as simply "serving the American society." On each of these points the correct analysis is considerably more complex, and complex in ways that bear directly on a proper understanding of professionalism for the future US military.

What Are Professional Obligations?

A few preliminary remarks are in order to avoid misunderstanding. There is no question that military members are obligated to follow the legal orders of their superiors and to serve American society as the society's civilian leaders see fit. Self-evidently, civilian control over the military means that the military does not pick and choose its own missions. The essence of the soldier's commitment to service entails the unlimited liability clause that he or she may be required to sacrifice life and limb in following those orders and striving to complete legally assigned missions.

In all those ways, the commitment (especially the voluntary commitment) of the soldier to selfless service of the society and dutiful obedience to constitutionally valid authority is the root of the nobility of the profession, and the source of American society's trust in and respect for its profession of arms. Indeed, it is for these very reasons that any overt affiliation of the vast majority of the military with a single political party is cause for concern. It is why endorsement of political candidates and causes by prominent retired officers using their military reputations for political purposes

is potentially damaging to the public's perception of the professionalism of its officer corps.

But having said all those things, one cannot take the view
expressed in the quotation above and retain any meaningful sense
in which military officership truly is a profession. Obedient service
is a crucial element of military professionalism, granted. Further,
there can be no question that at the end of the day the soldier's
obligation comes down to that: to follow legal orders, even if he or
she believes the orders to be misguided, foolish, and likely to cause
his or her death. But leaping directly to this "bottom-line" reality of
the military life not only fails to articulate what is important about
the military as a profession, but also actually eliminates the very
space in which the exercise of professionalism can and does occur.

Intellectual independence from the society is the essence of
professionalism, and not at all evidence of a lack of it. It is the
essence of a profession that members possess unique knowledge and
the skill to apply that knowledge to a given range or sphere of service. A formulation such as that above, with its exclusive emphasis
on obedient service, undercuts the centrality of the "abstract
knowledge" aspect of Abbott's (or any other) model of professionalism. As Friedson puts it, "Professionalism entails commitment to a
particular body of knowledge and skill both for its own sake and for
the use to which it is put."[9]

In another essay, Snider and Gayle Watkins acknowledge the
importance of professional expertise. Discussing the possibility that
"the Army should be allowed simply to deprofessionalize, becoming
an obedient but nonprofessional military bureaucracy," they list as
one of the "two key benefits" of a professional military "the development and adaptation of military expertise."[10]

The tension between this formulation and the one by Snider,
Nagle and Pfaff cited above on pages 60–61 is one of the central
issues in correctly defining "professionalism". How does one correctly capture the inherent intellectual component of professionalism and expert judgment without overstating it and suggesting
insubordinate or disobedient behavior based on that level of expert
knowledge, which is presumably superior to that of the military's
civilian masters?

If military officers are not, in fact, in possession of a body of
knowledge that constitutes the intellectual component of their pro-

fession, the idea of "professional military advice" becomes meaning-less. On that view, the skill and wisdom about how to employ mili-tary forces reside not among military officers at all, but among those who use the military as obedient tools, employed for ends beyond the purview of military officers themselves.[11]

But clearly this is not the case. Military personnel, and espe-cially officers, undergo extensive periodic education and training designed to impart professional knowledge and expertise, and they practice the application of that knowledge at all levels of their work—from field training exercises, through National Training Center rotations, to strategic exercises and war games. The result of that extensive professional development is, indeed, a degree of intellectual independence from the society they serve, and it is grounded in their unique professional focus.

The question of army professionalism is wrongly framed by the suggestion that intellectual independence is somehow inherently unprofessional or even threatening to civilian control in a democ-racy. The proper question is not whether there is professional intel-lectual independence, but rather how the intellectual independence inherent in the very concept of professionalism is properly exercised. But this is just to pose the issue, not to resolve it.

Consider a circumstance in which professional military advice has been rendered but not accepted by the professional's civilian superiors. Here the officer must decide whether this is the occasion for obedient service and deference to civilian leadership (the normal case) or whether the course of action chosen by political leadership is so at variance with sound professional judgment that conscientious resignation should be entertained as a possibility.

Unwillingness to render obedient service to policies an officer considers deeply flawed and utterly at variance with sound profes-sional judgment is not evidence of a lack of professionalism but rather a high manifestation of it. Indeed, the very essence of a pro-fession (as distinct from other occupations) is that the professional does possess and exercise independent judgment.

To cite Friedson once again:

[A]nother critical element of work that nourishes profession-alism lies in the nature of the relationship between client and professional. . . . In the case of employment in large-scale organizations we can put it crudely as whether or not policy is that customers are always right and that the organization and its members exist solely to serve, even cater to, their desires as long as they are willing to pay. Is the policy to provide what-ever customers or clients desire, even if their capacity to eval-uate the service or product is seriously limited and what they desire contradicts the better judgment of the professional?[12]

One of the most widely read and valued cautionary tales in contemporary US military literature is H. R. McMaster's *Dereliction of Duty*, a historical analysis of the relation of the Joint Chiefs of Staff with the Johnson administration during the Vietnam War.[13] The main point of McMaster's treatment is to demonstrate how the Joint Chiefs failed to deliver professional military advice to President Johnson regarding the conduct of the war in Vietnam. The book is widely read among the officer corps, not primarily because of its historical value, but, rather, as a morality tale on the lack of military professionalism on the part of the Joint Chiefs. According to McMaster's account, the primary moral failure of the senior officers was that they did not effectively exercise their intel-lectual independence and insist, to the point of resignation if neces-sary, that their professional military judgment be heard and accorded due weight by political leadership.

Of course, it goes without saying that it would be unprofes-sional in the extreme to appear to accept the guidance of political superiors and then to subvert it through less than enthusiastic implementation or downright evasion of the spirit and letter of the order. But of more practical concern, it is the attempt to "have it both ways"—maintaining one's status as a serving military officer while simultaneously being insubordinate to duly constituted lead-ership—that makes conduct unprofessional, not the intellectual independence of the professional.

It is this aspect of the issue that the Snider, Nagl and Pfaff quo-tation above on pages 60–61 correctly captures—that is, the obser-vation that "hesitancy" to accept missions assigned by civilian authorities is a cause for concern regarding army professionalism. But in order for the analysis to portray the problem accurately, we must assess the causes of the hesitancy. Insofar as hesitancy derives from application of the profession's body of knowledge, the root problem may not be solely the willing obedience to authority that is part of the essence of the military profession. In addition, it may derive from the changing character of the missions being demanded and, arguably, from the profession's legitimate concern that it is being tasked beyond existing resources and professional competency.

When professionals are asked to perform tasks that lie beyond their scope of training and competency, they may very well hesitate for good and professional reasons. A medical analogy would be the demand that a general practitioner of medicine perform coronary bypass surgery; a legal analogy, the demand that a personal injury attorney take a bank fraud case. Thus, before we draw the simple deduction that hesitancy implies lack of professionalism, we should explore the possibility that prudent disinclination, like intellectual independence, may be a manifestation of professional seriousness, not of a lack of it. We would not think well of the professionalism of the general practitioner who attempted a heart bypass; perhaps we should at least pause to reflect before we assume that the combat arms officer reluctant to take on police missions is culpably resistant to authority.

These observations point to the problematic nature of the third point raised in the Snider et al. quotation: the proposed definition of the army professional's core and defining obligation. The authors suggest simply that service to society is an adequate description of that obligation. But this cannot be an adequate definition of any profession's obligation. It stresses only the social dimension of professional obligation without giving equal weight to the way professionals must define their own body of knowledge and have their own highly developed internal sense of the proper application of that professional knowledge.

To say that physicians, lawyers, or ministers exist to serve society is, of course, correct. But to infer therefore that they have an obligation as professionals to collect trash or serve as school crossing guards, should society ask that of them, is ludicrous.[14] The point of these examples is that simply serving society's requests can never be an adequate definition of the obligation of any profession (although one might imagine a nonprofessional defined as a universal factotum of the society).

The reason it cannot be adequate is that it neglects the profession's own internal dynamic in assessing its body of knowledge, determining its relevance to a given identified social need, and negotiating jurisdictional questions with the larger society. The essential point here is that it is a multilateral negotiation, not a unilateral one. In an occupation, the hiring party can define every detail of the nature, scope, and method of the work, and then hire individuals willing to perform that work on those terms. Garbage collectors do not arrive on the job with a body of professional knowledge about the manner and scope of their work. In a profession, however, the case is different. The professional brings his or her own superior sense of the scope and limits of professional expertise to the negotiation. If professionals do not possess that sense, then they "are no longer able to exercise the authoritative discretion, guided by their independent perspective on what work is appropriate to their craft, that is supposed to distinguish them."[15]

Of course, the society may confer legitimacy on a profession or remove it. It may, for example, decide that chiropractors or Christian Science practitioners or acupuncturists are, or are not, "health care providers" for the purpose of insurance coverage. It may decide that some ancient and well-established bodies of "professional knowledge" confer no legitimacy on the supposed professionals (e.g., astrologers) even though some individuals and groups may continue to treat them as if they were professionals.

Having cleared some ground on the issues, we will now turn to the central questions: What is the essential nature of professionalism in the United States Army? How, in the present, ought that profession to be reconceived to adapt to the new social, cultural, and geopolitical context within which the contemporary army functions?

Toward a Normative Account of Military Professionalism

A normative account of professional officership can be defined in terms of the following major elements: professional knowledge, professional cohesion, and professional motivation and identity.

Entry into any profession is a kind of initiation into a body of knowledge primarily, if not exclusively, generated, transmitted, and built upon by fellow members of the profession. New members become familiar with that body of knowledge, learn where the major energy of the field is currently going, and, ideally, aspire to contribute to it as they join the ranks. As one comes to think of oneself as a member of the profession, one increasingly acquires a familiarity with its technical vocabulary and knowledge, and acquires the ability to speak its technical language with facility. One learns the identity of a pantheon of archetypal members of the profession and stories of their contributions to the profession. One becomes familiar with a set of institutions, awards, honors, and so forth, that members of the profession know and value (and that generally individuals outside the profession do not). One picks up, almost unconsciously, the small signals in dress, attitude, speech, and so forth, that members use to signal to one another that they are members of the same professional group.

It is also important to note that, in most professions, there is a core group of "real" members of the profession who have fully imbibed this knowledge. But there is also a large penumbra of para-professionals, who are knowledgeable in some areas essential to the profession's jurisdiction, but only some. To use medicine as an example once again, phlebotomists and X-ray technicians are essential to the core functions of medical care, but clearly are not members of the medical profession in the fullest sense.

One is tempted to suggest that the kinds of missions being assigned to the post–cold war army may seem to many in the profession as not calling upon and exercising core professional competencies. For example, the kinds of units that are required for effective operations in Bosnia and Kosovo are civil affairs and military police units, which are in short supply and are found largely in the reserves. The logic of "task effectiveness"[16] suggests that the active-duty army ought either to convert a significant number of its combat units to civil affairs and military police functions or to rather explicitly renegotiate jurisdiction issues regarding those functions with the society the army serves.

Resistance to doing so would be considerable, and for understandable reasons. In a particular health crisis one might find that the demonstrated priority need is for low-technology public health workers and perhaps family practitioners. No matter how true and strong that objective demand, however, one could predict that surgeons (for example) would resist being asked to fulfill those roles. It is important to understand the nature of that resistance.

The nature of professional commitment is complex. True, surgeons have a shared commitment to patient care and welfare. But they have invested years of training, reading, and practice in acquiring extremely technical knowledge and in learning its application. While from a certain level of generality all this is in the service of patient health and welfare, one simply cannot leap from that to the conclusion that it is the professional obligation of surgeons to retool their professional work. To understand the group and individual psychology of the profession, one must come to grips with the tremendous personal and societal investment in their identity and expertise, not merely as health care workers, or even as generic physicians, but as surgeons.

It is not adequate in describing this phenomenon, therefore, to focus only on the grand organizing purpose of the activity in patient welfare. One must also see the degree to which mastery of complex skills, equipment, and abstract knowledge has become embedded in the very sense of self of the surgeon. One can predict with certainty that surgeons asked to care for patients in ways that do not draw on those skills (no matter how effectively they treat the patients) will experience professional disillusionment, lowered morale, and diminished sense of commitment to the profession. The point would be equally valid for the "strategic leaders" of surgery as a profession in the face of a societal demand that their profession make such an adaptation.

One might be tempted to call such a reaction "unprofessional." After all, is not the essence of the medical profession a willingness to serve health and the welfare of patients? At some level, that is correct—and in the circumstance described. If the objective need is for the kinds of professional skill outlined, what is occurring is indeed what Abbott would call a jurisdictional dispute. Moreover, should surgeons persist for a long period of time in their own internally defined sense of professional identity, their skills might become less and less relevant to the health needs of their society, and their profession might wither and perhaps even die because of failure to adapt.

But clearly it is reasonable for at least a period of adjustment to occur. During that period, the profession collectively and surgeons individually would have to engage in some serious self-reflection and examination of their motives. Is their commitment to patients and health indeed their fundamental motivation? Or is the love of their specific set of skills and knowledge as surgeons in fact the foundation of their identity?

Before their profession was undergoing challenge, of course, that was not a forced choice; they could have both, in the confidence that the skills they took professional pride in mastering did indeed serve the well-being of patients. But now, in changed circumstances, what had been a happy convergence now becomes a hard choice.

Furthermore, the profession may be so conservative, so wedded to its earlier self-understanding, that the client comes to lose faith and patience, and simply withdraws jurisdictions from the profession, awarding them to more flexible or newly minted groups willing to meet the demands of the changed situation.

It may be the case that an analogous phenomenon is occurring in the contemporary army officer corps. Officers who have invested their lives and careers in mastering complex combat arms skills in particular branches of the army (infantry, armor, etc.) do experience professional disorientation when they are continually asked to execute missions that draw little, if at all, on their body of knowledge and its application. Yes, of course, they understand that their function is to serve the nation selflessly. But their entire sense of professional identity has been formed by stories of great combat leaders, heroic figures who sacrificed themselves in battle for the good of country and comrades.

Other communities and professions have different symbols, different archetypal stories, of course. But it is understandable that professional soldiers, newly tasked with peacekeeping missions and humanitarian aid, often react by thinking, "This is not what I signed up for." It is understandable (even if not finally defensible) if their traditional symbol system and narrative of heroic self-sacrifice cannot justify death and injury on such missions—and that force protection thus emerges as a high value.

Of course, like the surgeons in the example above, it may turn out that the objective need of US society is for sustained capability to engage in operations other than war and not for the the skills associated with more traditional combat arms. If that is the case, and if the army is unwilling to embrace the missions and come to embrace the professional knowledge required to engage in them, the profession will fail in the competition for jurisdiction.

It is far from self-evident what will happen at this historical juncture. Just as surgeons, individually and collectively, would face some hard choices in the scenario suggested, so would the officer corps. Assuming that some effective combat arms capability is a perpetual societal need, the army may choose to make the case that the preservation of such capability is the essence of its understanding of military professionalism.

If it takes that position and upholds it successfully, the army should be prepared to be radically downsized, unless and until it is necessary to build up a significant combat force when large-scale combat looms again on the horizon. This pattern is, of course, traditional in American military matters—the period of the cold war was quite anomalous in American history, given our customary suspicion of standing armies.

One should be leery of dismissing this possibility out of hand. Surgeons might well decide it is ultimately more important for them to maintain the purity of surgery as a profession than to maintain "market share." Some surgical skills will remain necessary, they might argue, and leave it to others to provide public health and general practice medicine (or in Abbott's terms, cede the jurisdiction).

So, too, army officers might decide that they are willing to pay the price of reduced force structure and funding in the name of preserving the knowledge and skills central to the core functions of combat arms.

In that circumstance, if the society remains committed to conducting operations other than war, it will necessarily constitute a force for that purpose. Inevitably, some subset of military skills (organization, logistics, etc.) will be necessary to carry them out efficiently. But the agents who conduct them may wear different uniforms, share different symbols, venerate different heroes, and understand their professional motivations in fundamentally different ways than combat professionals do.

In other words, the issue is wrongly framed as "professionalism" (which would counsel universal obedience to "the client's" demands) versus "unprofessionalism" (which resists some demands as beyond the sphere of professional expectations). Rather, it is an intellectual and leadership challenge within the profession. Is the profession of arms—having gained, transmitted, built upon, and capitalized upon a specific body of knowledge and its application in a particular form of expertise—flexible enough to choose to remake itself and compete for a new jurisdiction that requires different skills and bodies of expert knowledge?[17] This is the fundamental question before the profession at this historical juncture.

Professional Cohesion

Another central feature of a profession, as distinct from a mere occupation, is the ways in which individuals identify with it and with their fellow members. As Friedson says:

> [T]he social organization of professions constitutes circum-stances that encourage the development in its members of several kinds of commitment. First, since an organized occu-pation provides its members with the prospect of a relatively secure and life-long career, it is reasonable to expect them to develop a commitment to and identification with the occupa-tion and its fortunes....Second, since an organized occupa-tion by definition controls recruitment, training and job characteristics, its members will have many more common occupational experiences in training, job career, and work than is the case for members of a general skill class....Such shared experience. . . . may be seen to encourage commit-ment to colleagues, or collegiality.[18]

There is considerable evidence that the contemporary army offi-cer corps is experiencing difficulty in this dimension of the evolving profession. Study after study shows a deep distrust between levels of rank and status in the profession. Mentoring of junior officers by their superiors, even of the most minimal sort, such as discussion of annual formal evaluations, is lacking. The mere suggestion that colonels and captains are in any sense of the word "colleagues" would be met with derision in the contemporary officer corps.

One might say that formal aloofness between ranks is inevitable in a rigidly hierarchical profession such as the military. But this would be false. The relation between senior attending physicians in teaching hospitals and their interns is every bit as hierarchical as that in the military; and senior partners of major law firms are without doubt as superior to their junior associates as senior military officers are to their subordinates. In both cases, the professional fate of junior members of the profession is very much dependent on the assessment and evaluation they receive from their seniors.

Yet clearly law and medicine are more effective at instilling a sense of shared membership in a single profession than the contemporary military is. It seems equally clear that most junior physicians and lawyers identify senior members of the profession whom they admire and strive to emulate, and in some cases look to for mentoring. Other professions find mechanisms (Medical Society committee work, formal dinners, and law firm social events) that allow and encourage engagement between junior and senior members on grounds of collegiality.

At their best, professions instill and express the sense that all members of the profession are part of a continuous professional chain, linking the developing body of knowledge, expertise, and institutions through time. For the US Army, the "long gray line" has at times been a felt reality of the profession, providing an emotional and psychological sense of continuity and connection between the generations of officers. While many contemporary officers do feel that continuity, it seems clear that something has diminished it in the contemporary state of the profession.[19]

There is much anxiety and not a little confusion in the contemporary army about the professional connection between senior and junior officers. Sometimes it is expressed in terms of generational differences, sometimes in terms of respect and trust between age cohorts.[20]

Each of these perspectives is relevant to understanding the challenges to professional cohesion and retention of officers. But the root problem lies in something more fundamental and attitudinal. There is no substitute for the fundamental mind-set that members of the profession, regardless of rank, are colleagues, engaged in a common enterprise that matters deeply to them. If that mind-set is present, then each member feels a loyalty to the other, grounded in his or her common professional identity. If each thinks of professional identity in this way, each takes pride and responsibility in preserving, developing, and transmitting the body of knowledge that resides at the core of the profession.

Exactly this sort of engagement in a junior's professional development can be seen in Dwight Eisenhower's early career. During a posting as brigade adjutant in Panama, Eisenhower engaged in regular and extensive reading and discussion of professional literature with his commander, Fox Conner. One biographer, Geoffrey Perret, remarks, "Ike had always been exceptionally intelligent. What had been lacking until now was the time to read and the chance to talk over ideas with someone who was both a true intellectual and an accomplished soldier."[21] Perret attributes Eisenhower's intellectual awakening and deepened sense of the intellectual component of the profession to the fact that a senior officer and intellectual was willing and able to make it part of his responsibility to engage in professional development and dialogue with his subordinate.

Eisenhower's experience leads us to inquire about the presence of Fox Conner types in today's army. To what degree do senior officers in today's officer corps both model the profession as soldier-scholar and aggressively seek out promising younger officers to assist in the junior's professional development? Only the soldier-scholar preserves both aspects of truly professional officership: excellence in performance of military skills as currently understood by the profession and the contribution as a scholar to the continuing evolution of the body of professional knowledge that advances the profession through time. The United States Military Academy's strategic vision document well captures this essential dual requirement of the military professional. It states:

> While change is expected in any era of strategic transition, it nevertheless will severely test Army leaders. In order to serve the nation properly, the Army is pursuing an ambitious transformation agenda that will enable it to be strategically responsive and dominant at every point on the spectrum of operations—from actual combat to peacekeeping missions to humanitarian assistance. Forces will be more mobile, lethal, and agile, and better able to address the needs of our national security strategy. Leadership will also need to become more creative, able to cope with ambiguity, more knowledgeable about the intricacies of other world-views and cultures, more

aware of emerging technologies, and capable of adapting rapidly to the changing contextual realities of evolving missions. In preparing its graduates for this service, West Point will continue to assess and update its developmental programs, as it has done in the past.[22]

Were such mentoring relationships less rare, both the intellectual component of the professional and the bonds of trust between superiors and subordinates would in all likelihood be less problematic.

Professional Motivation and Identity

The fundamental questions of army professionalism turn on the precise nature of professional motivation within the officer corps and the flexibility of the personnel in adjusting to the new kinds of missions now being assigned to the military.

The relation between the contemporary volunteer military and American society can usefully be construed as an implicit contract.[23] Military personnel volunteer to serve the society in the application of coercive and lethal force. They serve on terms of unlimited liability, which means they follow lawful orders in full recognition that they may die or be severely injured in fulfillment of those orders. The terms of the contract may appear somewhat different, depending on whether it is viewed legally or morally. From the legal perspective, military personnel are obligated to follow all legally valid orders of their superiors. Morally, however, political leaders have an implicit contract with their volunteer military personnel.

The terms of the contract are that the military officer agrees to serve the government and people of the United States. He or she accepts the reality that military service may, under some circumstances, entail risk or loss of life in that service. This contract is justified in the mind of the officer because of the moral commitment to the welfare of the United States and its citizens.

Such considerations are critical in our assessment of professionalism, because they go to the heart of professional motivation and self-understanding. It is because of the ends to which their expertise and commitment will be devoted that officers are able to justify to themselves the grounds of their service. It is because they see themselves as engaged in defense of the values, security, and prosperity of their family and nation that their service has moral meaning.

It is not surprising, therefore, that in a time of greatly diminished threat following the demise of the Soviet Union, some of that moral self-understanding is undergoing challenge. The deployments in Kosovo and Bosnia raise additional challenges to professional self-understanding and motivation.

On the one hand, soldiers engaged in those operations generally report that they enjoy the opportunity to exercise their professional skills and abilities. On the other hand, precisely because the reasons for those deployments do not clearly link up to the moral core of professional self-understanding—that is, defense of the vital interests and survival of the American people and state—many officers worry that they are eroding their core war-fighting competencies and wonder whether such operations are "what they signed up for."

This particular understanding of the nature and purpose of the profession is not timeless. Rather, it has been forged in the remarkable and historically unique furnace of the cold war, especially the latter stages of the cold war when the military transitioned to an all-volunteer or all-recruited force.

For those who decided to make the military their profession during the cold war period, the threat was clearly identifiable and palpable, and the connection between their professional expertise and the defense of vital national interests was clearly visible. The Gulf War provided a manifest demonstration of the professionalism and competence of that cold war army, and to a large degree reinforced the professional values and assumptions that had shaped the reform of the army after Vietnam.[21] Having "grown up" in an army that took quite justifiable pride in that far-reaching reform and enhanced sense of professionalism, many officers naturally are reluctant to refocus their professional activities and self-understanding on activities ancillary to the war-fighting prowess that enabled that reform.

Perhaps the clearest expression of the connection between the war-fighting focus and the self-understanding of the profession is to be found in the Powell-Weinberger doctrine as insistence on overwhelming force, decisive victory, and definite exit strategies. To many officers, it seems to state immutable truth. But it does not, of course. Rather, as Suzanne Nielsen demonstrates, it is an attempt by the military to stipulate its own contract with society, the terms under which it is willing to be used, all in the guise of objective professional military advice.[25]

At root, however, the military does not set the terms of its social contract—certainly not unilaterally, and essentially not at all. As the times change and as the strategic needs of the nation change, the contract changes as well. As is made clear in the historical review of the profession by Douglas Johnson and Leonard Wong, the only real constant in military professionalism is that the military constitutes a "disciplined, trained, manpower capable of deploying to a possibly dangerous environment to accomplish a mission."[26]

The contemporary challenge of army professionalism is for the profession itself to engage intellectually with the changing nature of the environment and to embrace fully the need to lead in its own adaptation to that environment. The strategic reality is that large-scale land warfare is not on the immediate horizon of probability but that many other uses of disciplined forces the army can provide are.[27] Given this reality, it makes little sense to cling desperately to the self-understanding of the profession that was functional in the cold war. Neither can the US Army afford to accept other types of missions only grudgingly, while funneling as much energy and as many resources as possible into husbanding the capability for the preferred professional activity of large-scale combat.

What is required is for the army's officer corps to enthusiastically embrace the reality that the nation requires a different and more complex set of skills of its army today than defined it following the reforms of the 1970s. As with any profession in a time of change, it is psychologically understandable that a period of transition is likely as the profession mentally assimilates the changed circumstances.

But finally the profession must come to recognize that the wider and more complex range of missions the contemporary strategic context necessitates does actually fall within the profession's jurisdiction. In practical terms, that means the profession itself must apply its abstract professional knowledge to that range of problems and, when necessary, devote the intellectual work required to expand and enhance that knowledge. If new kinds of units, equipment, and training are necessary for the effective prose-cution of such missions, the profession itself should spend the polit-ical and intellectual capital to develop them.

The contemporary army transformation plan of crafting a lighter and more deployable force is a step in the right direction. But even that plan, still focused on large-scale land combat, will not be sufficient to address the widening range of missions the con-temporary environment makes likely. Admittedly, the contemporary scene is confusing, and it is difficult to foresee with accuracy every kind of new mission the army may be tasked to perform.

But some are clear: peacekeeping and peace-enforcement mis-sions will require larger numbers of civil affairs and psychological operations units. The assumption that units trained for high-end combat are really the most effective units to perform those missions is certainly debatable. Urban warfare and Special Forces operations against nonstate actors in urban environments are likely missions. Countering an enemy's use of various kinds of weapons of mass destruction looms on the horizon. It is an essential obligation of the profession itself to engage intellectually to determine how best to structure, train, and equip itself to perform those missions with the greatest degree of effectiveness.

Clearly, the army is aware that such missions are likely and is preparing, to some degree, to perform them. But equally clearly, they are viewed as secondary to the core function, which is large-scale combat (even with the future Objective Force, which will be lighter, more deployable, and more lethal).

The benefit of viewing professions through Abbott's lens is that it avoids viewing them statically and ahistorically. Rather, it sees professions as evolving through time in interaction with their envi-ronment and with other claimants to a given profession's jurisdic-tion. At the root of the challenge to army professionalism is the necessity to create and sustain the intellectual creativity to get ahead of environmental changes, to embrace them, and to demon-strate the intellectual flexibility to inspire the nation's confidence that it can meet the demands of the changing security environment with enthusiasm. Such a profession transmits and extends its corpo-rate culture and its developing intellectual engagement with a body of expert knowledge into the future environment.

Four

The Moral Role of Professional
Military Advice

Since the end of the cold war, the use of military force in international relations has entered novel moral and political territory. Increasingly, the humanitarian and human rights components of international law have emerged as a reason for use of force. Although humanitarian and human rights law experienced a considerable expansion after World War II, the filter of cold war rivalry largely blocked intervention based on it. Since the end of the cold war major powers have shown a willingness (most clearly in Kosovo) to use force in the name of human rights and humanitarian concerns. More traditional understandings of the sovereign right of states over their internal affairs have been trumped or overshadowed.

To what degree are we witnessing a genuine shift in the moral and political understanding of states and their relationships to their own citizens? Are we indeed witnessing the birth of a "new world order"? Will a universal understanding of human rights form the basis of a successor to the Westphalian system, which purchased international stability at the price of the religious liberties of individuals and established state sovereignty as the cornerstone of international affairs? Is the post–World War II promise that "never again" would the world stand by while massive violations of human rights occur about to be fulfilled?

Perhaps we are experiencing instead a passing moment of misguided international moralism. Perhaps it soon will become abundantly clear that the so-called international community lacks both
the will and the means to make such modifications to the practice
of international relations. Unless and until there is effective international authority with the military means to act consistently in the
name of universalizing principle, erratic, inconsistent, and piecemeal interventions may prevail rather than any genuine movement
of the world in the direction of greater enforcement of human
rights. If that is the case, the high moral talk of intervention will
only serve to increase cynicism. It may well soon become clear that
the so-called universal principles underlying intervention in fact
are invoked only in regions where powerful states are motivated by
ethnic affinity or thinly disguised national interest to intervene.

On the conduct-of-war side of the moral ledger, a wide range
of new military technologies (precision-guided munitions, air- and
sea-launched cruise missiles, global positioning receiver guidance
systems, unmanned aerial vehicles, over-the-horizon targeting systems, etc.) enable the military forces of the United States (and to
a considerably lesser degree, NATO allies) to use military force
with considerable accuracy and near-total impunity. Because of
these technologies, political and military leaders can use military
force in circumstances in which, in earlier times, they would not
have. Had they had only older technologies available to them,
interventions would have been perceived as too likely to produce
significant friendly casualties and therefore as too politically risky
to contemplate. Technology has reduced that threshold of concern considerably.

The existence of such technologies raises a number of novel
moral problems in their own right. Many have expressed the
moral concern that there is something inherently unfair in military conflict that is so completely asymmetric. Has the concern
with force protection gone too far in the use of NATO and US
forces—to the point of undermining the professional military
ethic itself?[1] Has the ability to use force with impunity lowered
the moral standard for the recourse to force considerably from the
last-resort requirements of just war? Does the ability to strike with
impunity from afar allow the US military in particular to be drawn
into conflicts in which it may inflict considerable damage while

remaining beyond the range of retaliation—but in the absence of a reasonable hope of success that military operations conducted in that manner will achieve the political and humanitarian goals of the intervention?

In the American democratic system, civilian leaders unquestionably make the final decisions regarding the use of military force. The president and the members of Congress are civilian leaders, answerable by popular vote to the electorate; the senior civilian cabinet officers serve at the pleasure of such elected officials. They bear the constitutional responsibility for deciding that a particular dispute warrants military action for its redress (i.e., meets the *jus ad bellum* requirement in just-war determination). The technical aspects of the use of force (the *jus in bello* dimensions of use of force) lie within the expertise of professional military officers. But because rational war-fighting is, as Clausewitz insisted, an extension of politics, even the rules of engagement and operational concepts of a given campaign are often influenced, if not controlled, by civilian leadership.[2]

In practice, military officers do play crucial roles in both kinds of decisions regarding the use of military force. This chapter will address general questions of the role of military force in humanitarian interventions. But it will do so from a particular perspective. Namely, it will treat the complex question of the role of the professional military officer and the place of professional military advice and expertise in assisting constitutionally established authorities to make such decisions wisely.

This discussion represents a subclass of the broader discussion about the nature and limits of professional military advice in a democratic political order. The challenge is always to acknowledge and respect two competing considerations: the genuine expertise of trained military professionals and the need to assure that their professional military advice is solicited and heard; and the vital concern to guard against the military's making claims to expertise that properly lies beyond the scope of military advice and encroaches on political expertise and authority.[3]

To capture the precise character of this issue in the contemporary scene, however, one must begin with an understanding of the rapidly evolving state of the relationship between US civilian and military leaders at this particular historical juncture. This time period is, by any standard, a time of great transition and a high degree of uncertainty.

As we noted previously, among professional officers one of the most commonly read books is H. R. McMaster's *Dereliction of Duty: Johnson, McNamara, the Joint Chiefs of Staff and the Lies That Led to Vietnam*. The common "message" of that book in the minds of military officers is the obligation of military leaders to insist that professional military advice is clearly articulated and, to the extent they can control events, heard and followed.

As the book's title would suggest, McMaster purports to demonstrate a very high degree of duplicity and unprofessionalism among the Joint Chiefs of Staff during the Vietnam War. In the minds of most officers, Vietnam was a clear case of civilians asking the impossible of the military, both in the ends sought by use of military force and in the civilian micromanagement of the conduct of military operations. The moral of the story of McMaster's book, at least as officers hear it, is "never allow civilians to manipulate military leadership and judgment in a similar way again."

The lessons the military thinks it learned about the relationship between military advice and civilian leadership from the Vietnam experience are largely codified in the Powell-Weinberger doctrine. As previously mentioned, so enshrined has this doctrine become in much contemporary military thinking that many officers believe it simply captures "professional military advice" in its own right.

But it is not in fact merely professional military advice. Rather, it is largely a set of rules of prudence and political judgments, few of which genuinely rest on unique military expertise.[4] In recent uses of military force, whether in Kosovo, Bosnia, or Afghanistan, it is not obvious what relevance the constraints of Powell-Weinberger have, other than the cautionary ones about thinking through the consequences of long-term deployments.

Whether peacekeeping or nation-building operations require continued presence of military forces for decades or generations (as in Korea and the Sinai) is not an issue of military expertise. Rather, it is a political and strategic issue as to whether the benefits to national interest and international security are worth the costs, literal and professional, of tying up military assets for such purposes.

For the post-Vietnam military, justifiably proud of its reforms in the aftermath of that conflict,[5] such uses of military assets fly in the face of the culture and professional self-definition of the military. What drove those reforms and made them successful in the army, for example, was a laserlike focus on large-scale, combined-arms war-fighting—precisely the kinds of rapid-maneuver armored warfare that Desert Storm showed the army to have mastered.

To suggest that troops trained for and culturally prepared to value such high-end combat skills should instead be used routinely for operations other than war seems to violate fundamental cultural assumptions about the measure of military excellence.[6] So does the suggestion that the military needs to reconfigure itself away from combat arms and create the much larger numbers of civil affairs, psychological operations, and water purification units necessary for really effective humanitarian interventions.

The key phrase in the minds of many officers, the foundation of their professional self-understanding, is that the army exists to "fight and win America's wars." Indeed, the former army chief of staff Eric Shinseki frequently referred to "fighting and winning America's wars" as "the Army's non-negotiable contract with the American people." Further, the disastrous decision to deploy ill-trained and ill-equipped US forces during the early stages of the Korean conflict generated another mantra: "No more Task Force Smiths." This slogan, in practice, means that forces must always be trained and equipped to win the first battles of any future conflict (not the pattern of most of American history, in which we lost the first battles and then eventually won when mobilization and industrial might were brought to bear).

From the longer view of American history, the conception that the purpose of military forces is to fight and win America's wars, is not typical. For much of our history the army has been used for a very wide variety of tasks, and only rarely for large-scale combat operations. Indeed, if one looks for any real constant in the nature and purpose of the American army, one finally arrives at a formula quoted previously: "disciplined, trained, manpower capable of deploying to a possibly dangerous environment to accomplish a mission."[7]

But as one approaches the question of the role of the professional military in rendering professional advice about the use of military force in humanitarian and human rights causes at the present moment, one must be aware that much of the U.S. military is culturally and professionally still heavily invested in a post-Korea and cold war self-image as a completely focused war-fighting military.

There is considerable discussion and increasing awareness that a different self-understanding and, indeed, a different mix of unit types and equipment than that created for the large combined-arms fight is needed, to accommodate the changed strategic environment. But one would fail to understand the contemporary civil-military dynamic if one did not grasp the depth of the transition required and the cultural resistance to that change.[8]

To state it most bluntly, the military has a significant resistance to embracing operation-other-than-war missions in general. This resistance is couched as disinterested "professional military advice." In fact, however, it relies on expanding the scope of claimed military expertise to include estimates of public support for the military and the clarity of the exit strategy. All of this is perfectly explainable in historical terms, of course: the "broken army" that came home from Vietnam was reformed by leaders who vowed that never again would America use her military in such an ill-advised way. That experience was so damaging to the institution of the military itself and to the bond between the American people and her men and women in uniform that senior officers understandably are deeply committed to avoiding such a breakdown in civil-military relations in the future.

To repeat, the particular constellation of training, force structure, equipment, and missions for which the US military has been structured in recent decades reflects a particular historical and strategic environment within which it was highly functional. But if the emerging international order is to bear little resemblance to that environment in the foreseeable future, clearly the military will need to rethink (or be forced by civilian superiors to rethink) its self-understanding and its view of its purposes in order effectively to render professional military advice to political leaders contemplating such missions.

The Role of Professional Military Advice in Use-of-force Decisions (Jus ad bellum/jus ad interventionem)

The decision that a particular set of political circumstances warrants a militarily coercive response is, of course, primarily a political decision. In the American system, such authority rests finally with the president in consultation with Congress. In the final analysis, therefore, the military is one tool available to political leadership for the achievement of national political goals.

While the military is a tool, it is not a mindless tool. The fundamental question before political leadership is whether the ends being sought can be achieved with the means available, within the political and ethical constraints and expectations of the American public and the world community. Military professionals, more than any other group involved in those decisions, possess the professional training and expertise to assess the suitability of the military means under their control for the successful achievement of the politically defined ends.

From an ethical perspective, the decision to use military force always bears the burden of proof. Even the most careful and judicious application of military force will cause the death and destruction of human beings and their property. Consequently, among the moral tests use-of-force decisions must meet is that there be a reasonable hope of success. In practice, this means that the use of force will be successful in bringing about the desired result with an acceptably proportionate amount of destruction.

Professional military officers possess expertise in judging the capabilities of the military instrument of power. Needless to say, the judgment that destruction of a given range of targets will bring about the desired political result is not a distinctly military judgment, but necessarily a political one—and one fraught with great uncertainties.

In contemporary military discussion, the term "centers of gravity" has come into currency. The term is systematically ambiguous, however. On the one hand, it focuses military planners on determining which targets are true nodes for essential enemy activities. For example, centers of gravity include structures containing the essential communication equipment for the adversary's military or the key nodes of an integrated air defense system. In this sense of the term, "center of gravity" possesses a fairly clear and objective meaning having to do with the connections among various systems available to an adversary and locating the most essential nodes in that system.

The idea of a center of gravity, however, also suggests that there is some mechanism of objective analysis by which military planners can determine which sets of targets are so vital to the enemy that destroying them will bring about the desired political ends. This differs from the first sense of the term in that it depends upon knowledge of the adversary's psyche and motivations—an inherently much more imprecise determination.

The first kind of judgment is clearly a valid military and intelligence function. In the case of the second, while such knowledge would be militarily highly desirable, gaining it is not really a matter of military expertise at all. At its core is a cultural and political knowledge regarding how a given set of targets rank in the enemy's culture and mind as compared with the political goals achieved by his continued resistance. In other words, it requires knowing how much pain to the enemy the destruction of a target is likely to cause, and how much pain the enemy leadership is willing to absorb before it will capitulate.

One need only review the history of efforts to demoralize civilian populations by strategic bombing to gain an appreciation of how difficult calculations of this sort can be in practice. How much pain an adversary is willing to endure in pursuit of a given political aim is inherently extremely uncertain. Obviously, an attempt to assess that determination must be made, both before entering a conflict (to meet the "reasonable hope of success" criterion of just war) and as the conflict continues (as one seeks to find the targets whose destruction will bring about capitulation or negotiation). But these attempts are not essentially informed by unique military expertise. While military expertise can advise that a given target can probably be destroyed with the forces available, the determination that its destruction is likely to produce the desired political result is more a matter of intelligence and diplomatic expertise than of military expertise.

This raises special challenges, especially in uses of force in pursuit of humanitarian goals. Generally speaking, the goals of the coercion do not extend to the complete and decisive military defeat of the adversary state, but only to a level of coercion necessary to bring about a change in specific behavior within the state. What is the proper role of professional military advice in such matters?

First, military professionals can offer an assessment of the probability that the military instrument in their possession, used within the constraints their political masters impose, will be able to meet or neutralize the adversary's military forces. Kosovo is an excellent example. While there was no question that the full force of NATO was vastly superior to the Yugoslav military, that was not the issue posed to military planners. Instead, the practical question was whether the use of NATO's air assets in a casualty-averse way (flying only above 15,000 feet, for example) would alone stop ethnic cleansing carried out by small, dispersed units of ground forces.

In this case, the overwhelming weight of professional military opinion was that it was extremely unlikely that such an "airpower only" campaign would be militarily effective, especially after Yugoslav forces had been given time to move into Kosovo, to disperse, and to gain covered positions. The air campaign planners were forced to employ their military instrument in a politically constrained way and to work down target lists. It was far from their ideal strategic air campaign, and ultimately, it was the requirement to continue bombing that pushed planners to go beyond the target set of which they had a good grasp. It resulted in the bombing of the Chinese embassy in Belgrade.

General Wesley Clark usefully describes his own thinking about the scope and limits of his role in advising on such matters at one point in the evolution of the conflict:

> A few missiles would make a political statement, but that was all. Then, too, a missiles-only approach couldn't hope to hit all the right targets. To me it didn't seem a wise way to proceed. On the other hand, such a strategy wasn't illegal or unethical. If nations wanted to fire a few cruise missiles to make a political statement, did I have the right to say they couldn't? I might argue against it, but there was no reasonable argument against just looking at a limited option.[9]

Clark's dilemma accurately captures the issue. The military officer has given a professional opinion, and considers the policy course being contemplated "unwise." Yet he is answerable to political leaders who, having heard that advice, are inclined to proceed. While the officer may have argued against the policy, so long as it is not "illegal or unethical" he is the instrument of that policy and is charged to carry it out.

In many respects, this view of the situation seems fundamental to the idea of civilian control over the military. For the officer to go further and refuse to execute the policy or covertly to undermine it in the name of his "superior professional knowledge" of military matters would, indeed, subvert the fundamental principle of civilian control of the military.

But by their very nature, humanitarian intervention operations depart markedly from the clarity of a "pure" military operation. They involve many agencies and nongovernmental organizations and have high visibility with the media, so there is little opportunity for the military to control that coverage. These realities make it virtually certain that civilian leaders will want and need to be deeply engaged in operational questions. Inevitably, this will pose challenges to civilian and military leaders to create a workable understanding of their respective roles.

The cautionary tale of Vietnam still looms large, however, in the minds of most officers, and rightly so. All believe that there is a point beyond which civilian leaders' management of conduct of war issues is going too far. When civilians reach deeply into the operational and even tactical level of military planning, they so subvert military officers' role as professionals that it becomes ethically incumbent on the officers to take great career risks to ensure that their advice is heard and heeded or, failing that, to resign or retire.

The role of professional military advice in these decisions is, then, necessarily complex and conflicted. Short of war, the issue is perhaps not *jus ad bellum* but *jus ad interventionem*.[10] *Jus ad interventionem* simply lacks the comparative clarity of well-thought-out theory that just war thinking can provide. Furthermore, military professionals are inevitably trained for, and have a strong preference for, the deployment of rapid, decisive, and overwhelming use of force to achieve unambiguous victory. This preference is so strong as to amount to a bias; and military professionals are tempted to equate the Powell-Weinberger doctrine's embrace of it with the essence of professional judgment itself.

But clearly it lies within the legitimate purview of civilian leaders to choose to use military force in ways that are not overwhelming, decisive, or even wise. Military professionals have the important responsibility to urge caution at such times. As the direct custodians of the health of their services' cultures and the lives of their soldiers, sailors, marines, or airmen, military professionals are rightly reluctant to send them on what they deem to be ill-considered missions. Further, being more familiar with the real dangers and suffering of war, military leaders have a livelier sense of the real meaning of combat operations in human terms, both for their own forces and for the adversary. Perhaps contrary to expectation, it is often the military professionals who are most loath to use military force.

Yet it is unquestionably a legitimate function of the civilian leadership to choose to use the military instrument of national power in ways that, to the war-fighting mentality of the professional officer, seem profoundly "unmilitary." For example, the stationing of US forces in the Sinai is clearly not a war, and it ties up significant military resources for decades. But they provide a security guarantee in a region where US interests require stability between Egypt and Israel.

To many military minds, such a use of military force is an undesirable drain on the forces and on their preparation for their "proper task." But because the military is a tool of the civilian leadership and its policies, such decisions are ultimately "above the pay grade" of any uniformed officer. The role of military advice in such matters is necessarily limited to explaining the costs of such deployments in money and availability of those forces for other important tasks and in sizing the force to be adequate to its assigned task. Whether those costs are worth paying is, all things considered, a judgment for senior political leaders.

The current security environment may, indeed, require a change in the military mind-set that has been dominant in the past fifty years. It may well need to rethink its capabilities and force structure so that it becoms a disciplined force available to civilian leadership to accomplish the difficult missions typical of the current international system. If such a fundamental rethinking does occur, future military leaders should be better prepared than current ones typically are to advise on the full range of interventions and uses of military force likely to arise.

The Role of Professional Military Advice in
Application-of-Force Decisions

I turn now to the other dimension of decision-making: regarding the "how" of using military force. The decision that a given set of political circumstances warrants application of military force goes hand in hand with a consideration of what degree of force will be used, in what manner, against what targets, and using which subset of the weapons systems available to the military.

The shadow of Vietnam casts its pall over this set of questions in the minds of many military officers, as it did over the *ad bellum* issues. Visions of political leaders choosing target sets and prescribing restrictive rules of engagement from the safe distance of Washington haunt the modern American military. Often, this is captured in the wish that political leaders would wholly restrict themselves to making the decision to use force in the first place and then get out of the way and "let the professionals" (i.e., military officers) determine all aspects of the operational plan.

While such a wish is understandable, and while it certainly contains a large degree of truth insofar as it cautions against unduly restricting operational and theater commanders from making decisions that make military sense, it is nevertheless not generally realistic. Only in a very large-scale war on the order of the Gulf War are political leaders likely to give the military a large degree of autonomy in conducting military operations. The lower one goes on the scale of peace and humanitarian operations, the greater the complexity one can anticipate in the intermingling of political ends sought, concerns for domestic political support, issues of media coverage and public reaction to it (the so-called CNN effect), and the military means employed. What role can and should professional military advice play in the dialogue about how to manage such a complex range of issues?

First and primarily, military advice serves to set a baseline for the analysis of any proposed intervention. Among the many voices in the policy debate, the military brings expertise regarding the limits and scope of what is militarily possible. Often a situation has percolated into the consciousness of the nation and political leaders only to the degree that there is a feeling that "something should be done" about it.

The military's special expertise is in providing decision-makers with clear indications of what the practical options are and what the foreseeable costs of various alternatives are in terms of lost lives and equipment. Military expertise is also well suited to estimating the effects of any given deployment on institutional military issues

such as the overall readiness of the force, recruitment and retention, morale, and public perception of the military. This is largely
because only uniformed leaders have welfare of the services and
units as their constant concern and focus. Military leaders are,
therefore, the custodians of the health of their services over longer
periods of time, whereas political leaders generally focus only on the
crisis before them.

To say the military possesses special expertise in such matters is
not, of course, to say it is infallible. History is replete with examples
of "expert military advice" that proved to be far too sanguine about
its capabilities. It can also be too gloomy. One need only read the
Civil War correspondence between Lincoln and General McClellan
to be struck by how Lincoln clearly grasped the proper utilization of
military forces in a way far superior to that of his military commander.[11] Still, in general, one should assume that military training and
experience provide knowledge regarding the proper employment of
military force to achieve a given set of ends, knowledge that political leadership ignores only at its peril.

Further, professional military advice plays an important role in
helping political leaders decide on prudent and appropriate means
for the use of force. It would appear there is genuine confusion
about these matters in the contemporary officer corps—so much so
that some have suggested that military professionalism itself is in
peril. Professor Don Snider, at West Point, has crusaded in the US
Army against what he perceives as a drift from military professionalism to merely obedient bureaucracy, and cites casualty aversion as
the major indicator of this drift.[12]

It is certainly the case that the trauma of Vietnam and the
damage it did to the services' internal culture, the development of
new classes of precision and standoff weapons, the concern with
the CNN effect, and the traditional sense of obligation to spare
one's troops combine to create the dream of a "riskless war."

There are numerous potential dangers if one believes in this
dream, however. For the decision-makers, the belief that they may use
the military instrument of national power with impunity inevitably
tempts them to employ it not as the "last resort" required both by the
ethical constraint of just war and by political prudence. Instead, they
may employ it almost as a first resort or without due regard to the fact
that risks are always inherent in military operations. Further, the

desire to use force risklessly may undermine entirely another important principle of just war and prudence: reasonable hope of success. We may find political leaders employing force in circumstances that generate no friendly casualties, but which do nothing to redress the political causes that may be at the root of the conflict: a truly desultory and futile exercise of military power. This is a phenomenon explored powerfully in Michael Ignatieff's recent book, *Virtual War: Kosovo and Beyond.*[13]

All these considerations point strongly to the need and responsibility of military professionals to make civilian leaders clearly aware of the risks (to our forces and to innocents) and the limits of the possible in any use of military force.

If a culture is allowed to grow up that makes prevention of friendly casualties a central priority or even a sine qua non expectation, there will be quite serious ethical and political risks for the military itself. For instance, the drive to protect one's own forces at all costs can lead military commanders to disregard entirely the ethical requirement to show due regard to the lives of the adversary, both military and civilian.

Personal experience of teaching ethics in warfare to senior military officers indicates that it is extremely difficult in the contemporary environment to get them to grant even the importance of the issue. The military's cultural expectation that overwhelming force will be used in all circumstances to ensure the maximal safety of one's own forces seriously threatens due regard to considerations of proportionality, military necessity, and discrimination in practice.[14] Such thinking risks swamping just-war considerations of proportionality and noncombatant immunity in tactical situations involving any threat, whatsoever, to friendly forces.

But even to raise this question is to recognize the difficulty of formulating correctly the nature of the professional military ethic. Obviously, it is inherent in military professionalism to "fight smart" rather than to "fight dumb." There is no glory or virtue in pointless and unnecessary loss of life and limb to the soldiers under one's command. It is testimony to the professional expertise of an officer that lives are not wasted and that advantages of terrain, equipment, technology, and timing are exploited to the detriment of the adversary. None of these concerns threaten professionalism by overshadowing the bedrock of military professionalism: mission accomplishment.

The essence of professional military judgment is the skillful and prudent expenditure of soldiers, equipment, and supplies in pursuit of mission accomplishment. Military officers are, in Samuel Huntington's famous phrase, "managers of violence."

To be effective managers, they must fully understand the complexity of the environment in which they do that managing. This includes a full recognition of the ethical, political, and diplomatic constraints that bear upon their decisions. It requires the maturity of judgment to grasp that while their world would be neater if political leaders would just define the mission and then get out of the way, that will almost never be the world within which they live and work out their professional obligations.

Part Two:
Moral Soldiers and Moral Causes: Serving the Needs of Justice in the New World Order

Five

Just Peacemaking: The Challenges
of Humanitarian Intervention

Just Peacemaking: Ten Practices for Abolishing War is a collaboration of twenty-three scholars, who tried to spell out in the book various practices that together comprise the essential elements of just peacemaking (JP). This chapter will not attempt a full-fledged assessment of the coherence, adequacy, and practical value of all elements of the JP proposal contained in that book. Rather, it will focus on the specific issue of the use of military force for humanitarian intervention.

This focus is worthy of attention because, as a practical matter, much of the debate in recent years has swirled around the question of what universal human rights are, and the question of how to gather political and military support to act on their behalf. It is precisely the persistence of such questions that indicates the importance of balancing the JP proposal with an equally robust framework for the justified use of military force in war, in operations other than war (including peacekeeping and peacemaking), and in the current environment in the far-flung "war" against terrorism.

Some misunderstanding of the JP proposals has been generated by the book's subtitle, *Ten Practices for Abolishing War*. Taken at face value, it would suggest that the authors believe that their practices cumulatively will indeed achieve such a grand effect. If so, then JP stands in sharp contrast to both pacifism and just war theory. In contrast to pacifism (at least the most profound kinds), JP would advocate quite vigorous engagement with the world of international affairs and foreign policy, and in contrast to just war theory it would dismiss the claim that there is an abiding and appropriate place for war (and other uses of military force) in morally legitimate statecraft.

Despite the talk about abolishing war, many places in the book (and subsequent work by Glen Stassen, the volume's editor), strongly assert that JP is intended to supplement and not to supplant just war theory. This chapter will argue that, just war criteria and JP's practices do in fact form a continuum of tools that can be employed, as practical wisdom and circumstances dictate, in pursuit of common moral aspirations in international affairs. After an overall assessment of JP's interpretation of the current international scene, this chapter will then turn to specific ways that JP can assist our thinking about humanitarian intervention.

In *Just Peacekeeping*, Michael Smith's advocacy of such humanitarian intervention is, by the editor's own admission, a position with which some of the other authors did not agree.[1] Yet his is the only chapter that deals directly with the issue of political/military power—the defining characteristic of the nation-state as it has evolved, and the central issue of the international order.

This suggests an important area for clarification in the JP proposal itself. While the volume *Just Peacekeeping* says at various points that it recognizes that war and the use of military force for purposes other than war will continue to be an important element in the international scene, it is perhaps less clear than it ought to be in demarcating the boundaries between areas of international life where the JP practices might usefully be applied and those areas where military force remains an important element of international agency.

This chapter will attempt to sharpen the discussion by exploring some of the areas of international life in which continued use of military force in pursuit of humanitarian ends serves the same ethical ends as those sought by the JP practices.

The Current International Scene:
Alternatives of the JP Proposal's View

A fundamental assumption of the JP proposal is that the post-cold war international scene is a time of unprecedented opportunity for new initiatives for peacemaking.

The interpretation of the international scene that underlies the JP consensus (including Smith's model of intervention) is resolutely internationalist and cosmopolitan. Drawing on the work of Paul Schroeder, the contributors share a belief that the direction of historical development points to an evermore interlocking international economy, a spreading network of nongovernment organizations, the strengthening of international authorities, and so forth.[2] These trends will create a world in which military force is rendered increasingly superfluous and in which its cost in proportion to any conceivable benefit will render it manifestly irrational—at least for large-scale interstate warfare.

Just Peacekeeping claims that the connection between traditional just war principles and JP is that the various JP practices "fill in the contents" of just war theory's "underdeveloped principles of last resort and just intention—to spell out what resorts *must be tried* before trying the last resort of war, and what intention there is to restore a just and enduring peace" (emphasis mine).[3] On this account, JP expands the repertoire of alternatives in advance of armed conflict and expands the scope of analysis of just settlement of those conflicts (and just international arrangements generally).

As a practical action guide, the requirement that in any and all circumstances these practices must actually precede use of military force seems imprudent and unwarranted. The absolute requirement that they be tried before force is used is asserted without any justification. While it is important, of course, to be sincere and honest about the last-resort criterion, the idea that any "checklist" of absolute requirements can capture the judgment of practical wisdom for all cases is on the face of it almost certainly misguided. It would make ethical reasoning much simpler, of course, if there were such a checklist, but in any real-world conflict, men of good will are always apt to disagree about whether the last-resort criterion has been sincerely respected.

Michael Smith's picture of the emerging world, while also quite idealistic, is fundamentally different than the dominant one held by the JP "consensus." Perhaps because he is grounded in the discipline of political science rather than in theology, his perspective is to some degree closer to the real world of political decision-makers. Rather than a freely cooperative and peaceful world, Smith's vision retains a prominent place for the coercive role of military power. His ideal world is one of states of diminished sovereignty. These states increasingly cede authority to a much-strengthened United Nations. The United Nations, so reorganized, possesses a volunteer military force prepared to intervene in the name of human rights globally.

Smith's is a picture of universal values and rights wedded to a universal political structure possessed of the power to impose by force the values of the international community. It would intervene to stop the kind of egregious massacres and violations of human rights that have occurred in Rwanda, Somalia, and Kosovo, and it would combat individuals and groups that attempt to act at variance with consensus international values.

Sharing a vision of the objective with his fellow JP scholars (increasing respect for human individuals, their rights, democratic government, economic prosperity), Smith still presumes that there are many actors on the world stage ready, willing, and able to bully their neighbors; and there are perhaps "irrational" actors (at least as the emerging global consensus understands "irrational") prepared to develop weapons of mass destruction for use against foreign enemies or against their own people.

For Smith the fundamental moral question is not "Military force or no military force?" Rather, it is "Force for what ends and under what authority?" He believes that national sovereignty no longer rules the international scene, and that it should be replaced with a much-strengthened United Nations. Not surprisingly, Smith's "muscular" international community would vary considerably from the model of peaceful cooperation that is adapted by most of the other authors of the JP project.

One might argue that the difference in perspective is also a difference in time of intervention. JP might assert that its practices would, if engaged in sufficiently early and with sufficient resources, be capable of obviating virtually all need for the use of military force, but still maintains that there will frequently be situations where such early and aggressive JP was not practiced and the situation was allowed to erode. Then the stark alternatives of standing idly by or using coercive military force for humanitarian ends could be the sole option. If one reads the JP proposal in this way, it offers a comprehensive model of conflict avoidance in theory, while recognizing the real-world limitations that will keep its practices from being deployed consistently and in a sufficiently timely manner to be effective in all (or even most) cases.

Alternatively, one might hold that JP's practices might not work at all in certain intractable conditions, and whether one intervened early or late. Then, too, coercive military power would remain the sole effective instrument. This interpretation (which I believe is Smith's) gives greater scope to the perversity of human nature, to irrational and evil actors on the international scene, and to the inherent limitations of knowledge and resources that will keep JP's practices from being effective with consistency and regularity on the international scene.

It is important to note, however, that from the perspective of many "realists" in political science and international relations, Smith's humanitarian world order is itself often viewed as unduly optimistic and overly enthusiastic about the capacity of international organizations. Smith's vision expects a degree of "felt cosmopolitanism" among powers that I doubt to be present now or likely to come about any time soon. While UN peacekeepers have performed a most valuable service in separating willing parties and defusing potential conflicts when the parties wish them to be defused, a UN force capable of forced entry and peace enforcement against a militarily significant unwilling party would require a level of interoperable equipment, training, and logistics very hard to imagine the UN attaining in the foreseeable future.

In the absence of a militarily powerful UN force, pursuit of the internationalist agenda will be left to the military forces of willing sovereign states and regional "coalitions of the willing." While Smith and Schroeder are certainly correct in noting the diminution of the power of sovereignty in many areas of contemporary international life, control of military forces is one area where it remains robust. Pursuit of humanitarian intervention in this political environment will inevitably be piecemeal. It will be substantially intertwined with the national interests of the interveners, and frustrating to all who, like Smith, wish to see universal principles backed up with consistent uses of military force.

Indeed, if one wishes to see relatively consistent and effective use of military power for humanitarian ends, one should be very reluctant to make the "right authority" in such matters to the UN as it exists now or for the foreseeable future. That would be a recipe for inaction in many of the most urgent cases imagined by Smith and other advocates of intervention.[4] The veto power of the permanent members on the Security Council would block proposals in which a major power had a stake (witness the problem of authorization for Kosovo). If one wanted frequent and effective humanitarian interventions, better candidates would be NATO and other regional alliances, to operating under the umbrella of general international agreement. Because of proximity or common interest, such alliances are more likely to be motivated and to possess the kinds of military forces and logistical support necessary to execute the mission.[5]

In one important respect, however, the JP project's consensus is significant and broad enough to embrace both Smith's military interventionism and the dominant JP thrust toward nonmilitary initiatives: all the contributers assume the post-cold war world is moving into a more globalized future. Underneath the disagreement over the continuing role of military force lies a conviction that the vision of the Enlightenment of a democratic world system, linked inextricably by bonds of commerce and shared values, lies, if not in the near future, at least within sight.

Whether this is so is probably the deepest critical question one may raise about the entire project. A number of very astute scholars have written powerfully of a quite different future for the world. Instead of global village, they suggest, the future holds some stark choices: "Jihad vs. McWorld."[6] As these scholars survey the same set of facts as the JP scholars, they see not an emerging global society of shared values, but either a knife-edge walk between competing and incompatible visions or, even more grimly, a struggle to the death between utterly incompatible values and cultural forces—a clash of civilizations. Some see this as a moment in which "America sleeps" and fails to recognize the need for even more robust military forces and their more frequent use in pursuit of the strategy our sole remaining superpower status makes possible.[7] The terrorist attacks of September 11, 2001 clearly warrant a large-scale and far-flung use of military force to eliminate the sources of future attacks. The degree to which the international cooperation that characterized the early days of that conflict will continue is a complex matter not only politically, but (given the absolute disparity in capability between the United States and even its closest NATO allies) militarily as well. The unilateralist features of the decision to invade Iraq certainly, at a minimum, put pressure on that consensus.

What is the relevance of these quite different pictures of the future for the cogency of the JP proposal? At a minimum they raise a useful caution against a premature or too-enthusiastic embrace of a single vision of the possible/probable human future. There is much in the international scene that allows reading that future as the JP authors do; there is much to inform a far darker and more conflict-ridden vision.

There are many indications in recent years that the darker vision is most likely. But certainly in the aftermath of September 11, 2001, one should expect a serious hearing for these forecasts. It is, at very least, now abundantly clear that forces are at work that would, if they had capability, destroy the foundations of the emerging international order envisioned by any version of the JP proposal. Those forces stand willing to do so, even to their own destruction, and almost certainly with weapons of mass destruction if they had them. They are unlikely, to put it mildly, to be dissuaded by JP's practices.

JP at its root shares some assumptions very common in much of the academic community. For example, it assumes that the desire for human rights and democratic government is universally shared. In this worldview, there is a kind of "manifest destiny" for those political values, and expanded human rights, the globalized economy, and so forth are the wave of the future. In my opinion, this significantly underestimates the depth of the conflict and the hatred a realistic international policy must be prepared to confront.

What if, instead, the real-world situation is a struggle to the death between competing visions of human civilization and culture? What if, like the situation of the early Christians at the beginning of the fifth century, the question is not the triumph of moral idealism, but rather the persistence and success of the civilization itself? What if the price of military and cultural defeat is the loss of the cultural gains of millennia and the collapse of high civilization itself?

The JP project clearly rests on a particular interpretation of the historical moment. Of course, the reasons offered for that interpretation of the future are plausible. They are not fundamentally different from those offered by Immanuel Kant in the eighteenth century in his vision of "perpetual peace." Naturally, the vision of advancing into a peaceful, democratic, prosperous, and united human future is attractive. As an eschatological vision it is unassailable. Whether it provides useful practical advice here and now is more debatable, in particular if it blinds the individuals and communities that share it to very real threats that need to be dealt with immediately.

To his credit, Smith's proposal assumes only an emerging international consensus on what the human rights norms should be; and he does not assume that there will be no resistance to them. His conclusion that "a revitalized United Nations equipped with a standing volunteer military force"[8] is desirable does not specify that force's size or operational tempo. In my view, if it were to execute his vision of consistent action in defense of human rights globally and effectively, it would be very, very large, and very, very busy.[9]

Clearly, there is need for a metatheory that incorporates the important contributions of the JP practices but also provides clarity in thinking about where JP might be useless or inappropriate. Ideally, it would also frame use-of-force questions in a way that would provide guidance for coercive peacemaking endeavors and also for legitimate war-making employment of military force. Only with such a comprehensive vision can JP's proposals fit within a sufficiently realistic framework and avoid the hint of utopianism that otherwise might lurk, unwanted, in the JP proposals.

Given the frequent assurances of the authors of *Just Peacekeeping* that they recognize international conflict will occur and their insistence that they intend their recommendations to be practical and politically realistic, perhaps what is needed from a moral perspective is a moral principle that underlies practical engagement in worldly matters. "Use all elements of national and international power and cooperation so as to advance the cause of justice and minimize human suffering and loss of life" may be such a formula.

In some circumstances, that principle will counsel prompt use of overwhelming military force; in others, the cultivation of international cooperation and nonviolent means to advance those causes. Those inclined to reach for military means may often overlook alternatives and thereby violate the principle by increasing suffering and death; those inclined to place great hope in internationalism and cooperation may delay effective military action in hopes of finding alternatives, also to the violation of the fundamental moral principle. Knowing which situations call for which approach is the essence of practical wisdom.

*The Contribution of JP's Practices
to Humanitarian Intervention*

We turn now to the much narrower question of the contribution of JP's practices to humanitarian intervention. This question is premised on the assumption that military forces will be used to maintain peace when warring parties consent and to enforce peace and to prevent atrocities and the violation of human rights, even when the perpetrators do not consent. I leave to the side the questions of the frequency, consistency, and authority for those interventions. Given that the military has created a relatively stable and relatively peaceful environment where previously there was none, what is the value of JP's practices in improving our view of how to proceed? Alternatively, in circumstances where time and resources permit, what contribution can JP's practices make to forestall deterioration of a situation to the point that coercive means are the only timely interventions possible?

It is here that the practices of the JP proposal have the greatest immediate applicability. Time after time, the world has witnessed a military intervention that was extremely effective in "solving" the particular problem that justified the intervention (deposing a dictator, stopping ethnic cleansing, restoring deposed elected leaders to power). But once the military operations were essentially completed, the exit strategy and final disposition of the situation have more often than not been badly handled.

Because often it is the only well-disciplined force capable of maintaining order, the military is tasked to fulfill missions (e.g., law enforcement, food distribution, and health care) for which it is not prepared or that do not constitute the best use of its skills. Often the military is left deployed in an environment because no one knows how to restore civil society to the point that factions will not, on their own, resume killing each other. Still worse, at some point the sustained deployment may no longer be possible (politically, economically) or violence may be done to the military force and it is abruptly withdrawn (e.g., Somalia, and to some degree Haiti), leaving the country only marginally better off than it was before the deployment.

The JP practices of cooperative conflict resolution, independent initiatives for threat reduction, acknowledgment of responsibility, advancement of democracy and human rights, fostering of just and sustainable economic development, working with cooperative forces (NGO, UN, and regional), and reduction of the weapons trade (especially in small arms) all speak to this very real gap in humanitarian interventions.

Needed to fill the gap are well-trained and well-disciplined groups prepared to follow the military into these environments and capable of "taking the handoff" when military forces are no longer the appropriate instruments and "nation building" is the major remaining task. The distaste for nation building expressed in the 2000 presidential election stems from the valid perception that the United States and the world community lack precisely the "force structure" (to use the military term) to execute that phase of any humanitarian operation effectively. But the experience of Afghanistan also shows that it is impossible to exit when the central military mission is completed without undermining the moral justification of the entire intervention or even its long-term political success.

If the practical effect of JP's practices is to create such organizations and units, it will have provided an essential element for truly successful humanitarian interventions. Indeed, governments and international organizations might be more willing to use their military forces for humanitarian interventions (as Michael Smith wishes they were!) if they knew that there would be competent, well-trained, well-disciplined nation-building forces ready to take effective charge when their military missions are complete.

Needless to say, those forces would have to be willing and able to link up tightly with military forces, to gain the respect and trust of military and civilian leadership, and, perhaps, to be prepared to take casualties in execution of their mission. At present, some of the most effective groups in these areas are NGOs—although the appropriate UN agencies are important, and their effectiveness and funding could be increased as well.[10]

US citizens have a way to participate directly in this. Groups and individuals who take seriously the importance of JP's various practices might advocate a policy that the US government fund and build deployment capability into other federal departments and agencies. To cite only a few examples, why could not the Department of Justice be tasked, funded, and prepared to deploy for the rebuilding of legal systems? Why couldn't the Department of Agriculture be given the mission of deploying personnel in the wake of humanitarian intervention to help establish sustainable agriculture? Why couldn't the FBI have units trained, funded, and equipped to help reestablish effective local law enforcement? A useful model might be the recently developed Federal Response Plan, which delineates in great detail the responsibilities of the various departments and agencies of the federal government in responding to domestic disasters.[11] The Federal Emergency Management Agency takes the lead but has the assistance of the defense coordinating officer, who draws on Department of Defense assets to assist in coping with domestic disaster. A similar structure could be evolved to cope with international humanitarian intervention and nation building.

Similarly, nongovernmental teams skilled in the practices of cooperative conflict resolution and in facilitating acknowledgment of responsibility, repentance, and forgiveness may be absolutely essential in a conflict such as the one in Bosnia. In such deep-seated conflicts where memories are long, one suspects no amount of institutional rebuilding will ever bring a stable and just society if those more fundamental issues of inter-necine conflict remain just below the surface. This is, of course, precisely the kind of work David Steele (one of the participants in the JP conferences) is attempting in the Balkans. It is precisely the kind of cultural engagement that is necessary, and that militarily imposed order can, at best, only make possible. Because of the cultural sensitivity it requires, here is a place where JP NGOs are most likely to be the effective agents rather than US military or government entities. The challenge will be for the military to come to trust in the professionalism and dependability of such NGOs so that it views them as an asset in its overall pacification strategy. This is by no means utopian: witness the close cooperation between military forces and the Red Cross in addressing humanitarian concerns in modern conflicts.

JP's practices are indeed an essential augmentation of the short-term ability of military forces to intervene and provide the stability that is the precondition for addressing the underlying cultural, religious, and economic causes of the conflict. Here, the practices of JP are an essential contribution to the overall effectiveness of any policy that would move a given country, region, or the world, in the direction of a more peaceful and stable future.

Much of the judgment about when to deploy some or all of the practices of JP in a given situation will, of course, depend on where one "starts the clock" in one's assessment. Some situations cry out for immediate use of military force to bring a halt to the killing and massive violations of human rights. Others appear to be at the beginning of a process that, if allowed to evolve unchecked, would develop into situations that bad. In such cases, JP's practices may well be effective in preventing the descent into conflict. What is required here is, of course, practical wisdom and accumulated experience to determine what kinds of interventions, inserted at what point, can effectively prevent conflict. And military force will still have a place so long as the causes of international conflict persist.

We see, then, that it is critical to treat both JP and just war theories and providing tools in a large and complex toolbox available to leaders of nations, religious organizations, and NGOs. If the goal is to minimize loss of human life and suffering while increasing the respect for human rights, each of these tools (and various mixes of them) will be required.

The JP proposals contribute to the ultimate goal of giving political leaders and NGOs a full range of options. It is essential that JP's practices not be viewed as inherently preferable morally to just war theory's criteria for the use of force: both perspectives share a common moral imperative to act in realistic and practical ways to advance common moral goals.

JP's practices helpfully remind just war thinkers that there is a wider range of tools available, depending on circumstances, than they might ordinarily consider. At the same time, just war theory and alternative readings of the current world urge caution upon JP's perhaps unduly optimistic interpretation of the present situation.

Six

Resisting Global Terrorism

In this chapter, I wish to take the just war tradition in its developed form (as both a moral and legal tradition) and look at the particular moral and legal challenges raised by the unusual character of the current "war on terrorism."

The nature of this conflict raises issues and challenges that have not been faced by the just war tradition in a number of centuries. Consequently, the current letter of the law may prove to be less relevant to guiding our thinking about this challenge than the older and deeper philosophical and religious roots of the just war tradition.

Terrorism and the current just war framework

The just war framework, as we have seen, concerns judgment whether particular political circumstances justify recourse to military force. The tradition inherits from its Christian roots a strong bias against the use of force and a presumption that means short of use of force are in general preferable to military solutions to political problems. But it balances that bias with another: the presumption that evil should be punished and that stability and order must be maintained, by force if necessary.

The just cause aspect of *jus ad bellum* is meant to establish a threshold of gravity of offense sufficient to justify use of military force. As this tradition has developed, various things have been counted as just causes. For example, in the Middle Ages "offended honor" was considered a just cause. Because the intent of the tradition is to restrict the use of force, there has been a tendency, as the tradition has developed, to narrow the range of just causes. In its contemporary form, just cause is largely restricted to "aggression received." The simplest form of aggression would be when one country's tanks are on the wrong side of the border.

The requirement of right authority was initially meant to put a limit on private wars not authorized by a legitimate government. This was, of course, a real problem in the Middle Ages, since local aristocracy had private armies at their disposal; and it is becoming a real problem again as nonstate actors such as Al Qaeda also possess military power uncoupled from responsible governance structures.

In theory the creation of the UN restricts right authority to the Security Council of the United Nations except for absolutely and unambiguously defensive wars. The intent of the creation of the United Nations was to restrict warfare as a normal means of international resolution of dispute. In theory it ceded to the Security Council the authority to make determinations that conditions were threats to international peace and stability worthy of redress by military means. Naturally, member states of United Nations retain the right of self-defense, but, as just indicated this was restricted to unambiguous circumstances.

Within the United States, there are questions that remain about where right authority lies. As we all know, the Constitution provides that the president be the commander-in-chief of the armed forces of the United States, while reserving the power to declare war to the Congress. For much of our history, this division made sense, since the presumption was that there would be no large standing military force and that Congress would have to authorize money to raise an army to fight any significant war.

But the historical abnormality of the cold war left us with a different situation. Due to the urgency of the cold war threat and the need to have standing military forces ready to respond promptly, the president was left with a standing military force that could be deployed on presidential authorization alone.

Since the Vietnam War, Congress has attempted to restrain this unilateral authority of the president through the War Powers Act, but all presidents have held that the War Powers Act is unconstitutional, and neither the executive nor the Congress has chosen to force the issue by taking it to the Supreme Court.

Justification of the recourse to military force also involves a global proportionality assessment. This is a judgment that the gravity of the issue to be resolved is in some reasonable proportion to the amount of damage anticipated by the use of military means.

The reasonable-hope-of-success criterion is essentially a matter of common sense. Since the use of military force will inevitably involve destruction of property and probably cause deaths, any morally serious defense of use of force must be able to guarantee that such use is likely to be effective. Otherwise, the destruction is purely gratuitous.

The requirement that use of force be the last resort is the final criterion of *jus ad bellum*. The essential idea here is that if there are nonmilitary means of redressing the fundamental issue, they should be tried. This is not, of course, an iron-clad requirement that everything conceivable be tried. Instead, it is a common sense requirement that things that show any realistic promise of being successful should be tried. You will recall that this was the central debate in anticipation of the Gulf War: Would another trip by the Russians be effective in getting Iraq to withdraw from Kuwait? Was further UN negotiation likely to be effective?

The other wing of just war theory is *jus in bello*. Here we are invited to make judgments about how war is conducted. The central moral principles here are discrimination and proportionality. Discrimination concerns the accuracy of weapons and targeting. The idea here is that some individuals and targets are legitimate military targets, while ordinary civilians and infrastructure are not.

Military planners are morally obligated to choose weapons and tactics that as far as possible allow attack on the military targets while avoiding damage and destruction to the civilian populace.

Proportionality captures the common sense requirement that the amount of destruction visited on a particular object or site is proportional to the military value of the object.

Application of These Criteria to the War on Terrorism

While we have seen repeatedly in earlier chapters that these criteria have been the mainstays of just war thinking for many centuries now, there are some distinct conceptual problems in applying this tradition to the current engagement against terrorist organizations worldwide.

The first and most obvious difficulty is that the just war tradition since the Peace of Westphalia in 1648 has been organized around the principle of sovereign states. Westphalia allowed international peace in Europe by allowing each state to control its own internal affairs. In practice, this meant that Catholic states would persecute Protestants, and Protestant states would persecute Catholics. International stability was to be bought, as we would say in modern parlance, at the price of human rights.

Accordingly, only states can truly wage war against one another. Therefore, when we use the term "war on terrorism," we are not using language precisely. Of course, in the case of Afghanistan, the fact that the Taliban government of Afghanistan was unwilling to hand over the al Qaeda representatives within its territory made it possible to conduct war against the de facto government of Afghanistan, as well as against the terrorist groups whom they harbored.

But as our engagements with al Qaeda extend globally, the character of that engagement will change dramatically with reference to the various states in whose territory they may be found. Some states, such as Georgia, may invite American forces to operate with their own forces to suppress terrorist organizations they have internal reasons for wanting to suppress. Some states, such as Pakistan, may have governments willing to act to suppress and locate al Qaeda representatives, but at considerable domestic political risk to their own stability. Some states may be too weak, even if willing, to act against al Qaeda; indeed, some may actively support or covertly be willing to tolerate terrorist presence in their territories.

Given that complex picture, how do we begin to think about our relationship to these various situations? The modern theory of state sovereignty would counsel that every state is free to do within its own territory whatever it chooses. Presumably, that freedom includes harboring individuals and groups that are unpalatable to other states. But clearly, it is our intent to pursue al Qaeda wherever we may find it, even in the face of resistance or noncooperation from the government in whose territory its members may reside. What justification in terms of just war can there be for such interventions?

Obviously, there is no great ethical or legal question involved with states that choose to cooperate in our efforts. They are clearly acting within the scope of their sovereignty when they invite us to assist them in locating and defeating terrorist groups within their territory.

But what about those states that do not cooperate, either from inability or from unwillingness? The standard of Westphalian respect for territorial integrity and sovereignty would argue strongly against granting the United States or even a coalition the right to intervene in such circumstances—at least in the absence of an authorizing resolution from the UN.

But it may be that the era of Westphalian sovereignty is fading. Recall that the moral tradition of just war is much older and more robust than its particular instantiation in formal international law.

Recall that in his "Letter to Count Boniface," Augustine urges the Roman military commander Boniface to see his military service in resistance to barbarian invasion as a mournful but necessary duty. The necessity of fighting has been imposed by those who have disrupted the relative peace and order of the Roman Empire, and not by Boniface.

Writing from his home in North Africa to this senior military officer after Rome itself has already fallen, Augustine invokes Jesus's saying, "Blessed are the peacemakers," and applies it to the conscientious soldier who, by using arms against the barbarian, is attempting to restore the peace that has been broken by invasion.

The temporal peace Augustine urges Boniface to restore is not, by any stretch of the imagination, the perfect peace of the City of God. It is the lesser temporal order of the Human City—a "tranquility of order" in which there are still many who are miserable, but within an overall framework of order. Augustine grants that individuals in that order may be wretched but says "they would....be far more wretched if they had not that peace which arises from being in harmony with the natural order of things."[1] Augustine realizes that, in the conflict between the barbarians and the Roman army in his lifetime, the stakes are high: the survival or collapse of civilization as his world had known it. He realizes that what would follow if Rome were defeated (and what did follow, since it was!), would be not just a rearrangement of the individual miseries of his world. What would follow would be the Dark Ages, and centuries would pass before even a flicker of civilization would reappear in the Western Roman Empire.

What is the relevance of this ancient discussion to the current Global War on Terrorism? Like Augustine, we are now dealing with threats and challenges that do not fit the model of state sovereignty that has defined the Westphalian world for the past four centuries. What is threatened by al Qaeda is not captured in a conceptual model that thinks of wars as conflicts between states, or in which what is at stake is the prospering or survival of a particular state's political order or territory.

If al Qaeda's fondest hopes were realized, what would fall would not be the United States of America, but rather the entire world order created over centuries by the forces of capitalism, Enlightenment rationality, modern science, and political democracy.

It is fashionable, of course, to criticize the miseries created for many groups and nations by that world order. There are, indeed, many valid and important questions to be raised about the effects of globalized trade, the World Trade Organization, or the spread of American culture across the planet. And it is no more of the essence of the argument to idealize our civilization than it would have been for Augustine to have pretended that Rome ruled a world of sweetness and light. Moral seriousness requires, instead, asking, "If this civilization falls, what comes next?"

There is always room for reform and change under the umbrella provided by Augustine's "tranquility of order." The sober assessment of the situation asks not about the perfection of order, but about the cost of its collapse. One intellectual disease of much of modern liberalism and many a modern university is a kind of moral utopianism that one-sidedly dwells on the deficiencies and injustices of existing civilization.

Such a perspective neglects entirely to balance moral criticism of imperfections with an equivalent recognition of the value of order. Such thinking is then squeamish about the reality that such order is always maintained by power, often in ways that are less than perfect or ideal.

Such moral utopianism fails entirely to provide a moral and conceptual framework within which real-world political decisions can be made. One finds such views, for example, in perspectives that attribute responsibility for the attacks of September 11 exclusively or primarily to elements of American policy and conduct— while not recognizing the absolutely essential role of America and her power in maintaining what passes for "tranquility of order" in the modern world.

When one contemplates an absence of that order, few can improve on Thomas Hobbes's description:

> Whatsoever therefore is consequent to a time of Warre, where every man is Enemy to every man; the same is consequent to the time, wherein men live without other security, than what their own strength, and their own invention shall furnish them withal. In such condition, there is no place for Industry; because the fruit thereof is uncertain: and consequently no Culture of the Earth; no Navigation, nor use of the commodities that may be imported by Sea; no commodious Building; no Instruments of moving, and removing such things as require much force; no Knowledge of the face of the Earth; no account of Time; no Arts; no Letters; no Society; and which is worst of all, continuall feare, and danger of violent death; And the life of man, solitary, poore, nasty, brutish, and short.[7]

What I am suggesting is that we may well be at one of those historical moments when a real shift in our thinking is required. It is not the just war framework of the post-Reformation Westphalian order that provides the deepest insight to our circumstance— although the fact that black letter international law presupposes that order makes harmonizing our challenges with that form of the just war tradition necessary and important. But the terrorist challenges are not fundamentally challenges to particular states, but rather to civilization itself as we know it.

For all the brutality of its foundations and conduct, the Pax Romana was, for Augustine, clearly an order worth defending; no less, the Pax Americana in our time and place. Indeed, a striking fact about the early Christian church is that, for all its ambivalence about living under Roman rule, there was never the hint of a doubt that the stability, safety, and ease of travel made possible by Roman power was a gift of God. Similarly, it does not require much imagination to envision the human consequences of a collapse of the complex and interlocking structures of the modern international system. Of course, there is plenty of misery in our world, but it pales in comparison to the misery that would arise from an abrupt break or collapse in the structures that keep it intact.

The most fundamental point of the evolution of a just war perspective in the Christian church was a resolute embrace of the realm of practical politics as a locus of moral seriousness. The temptation to flee the world of moral ambiguity and shades of gray is, of course, a powerful one—a tug no morally serious person can avoid feeling. But it is, from the core of the just war perspective, a temptation to be resisted in favor of the hard, messy, and (as Augustine put it) "mournful" work of sustaining relative goods in the face of greater evils.

Seven

Noncombatant Immunity and the
Force Protection Imperative

"During the Kosovo crisis, pundits at home and abroad charged that the Clinton White House overvalued the lessons of Vietnam and Somalia, and underestimated the willingness of the public for a fight when it perceives important issues at stake. The result, they argue, was a military campaign devoid of daring—so fearful of its own losses that it could not save the Kosovar refugees or effectively punish Serb atrocities.[1]"

Contemporary American policy on the appropriate use of military forces reflects deep tensions. The common analysis, as the quotation above suggests, is that American political leaders have concluded that use of American military force will only be politically acceptable if American casualties are kept to a minimum. Partly in negative reaction to the prolonged agony of Vietnam (not to mention the debacles of Lebanon and Somalia), and partly in positive reaction to the apparently bloodless and very quick Gulf War, so the analysis goes, American society has accepted a new standard for acceptable military conflict: immaculate war.

This analysis has a large degree of truth. But there are deeper issues of ethical principle underlying the impulse to have only immaculate interventions. The impulse to intervene comes from one particular view of international order and of the role of the American military in that order, while the impulse to keep such interventions immaculate arises from the misfit between the interventionist impulse and the moral contract between political leaders and the men and women of the armed services who bear the burden of executing such interventions.

The Interventionist Imperative

American political rhetoric about military intervention has always been moralistic. To the constant frustration of political "realists," American political culture has been notoriously resistant to reducing intervention decisions to clear-eyed (and cold-hearted) assessments of narrowly conceived national interest. No matter how unglamorous the real motives of national interest, interventions as tawdry as the Spanish-American War, our repeated interventions in Nicaragua, or the recent invasion of Panama, have consistently been cloaked in high rhetoric and appeals to moral principle. American political discourse tends to speak in universalizing terms of the war to end all war, of advancing universal human rights and democratic political order, and of opposing tyranny and despotism.

So the fact that our interventions in Kosovo (and Bosnia and Somalia) are spoken of in terms of universalizing claims about the protection of the rights of individuals is not new. Yet it would be a mistake to take this moral rhetoric as merely masking realpolitik. The end of the cold war has created, at least for this historical moment, a time and space in which a genuinely new form of international relations seems possible. Whether that portends great moral progress in international affairs or is a mirage of great moral possibility that will lead to disaster is yet to be determined.

It would also be a mistake to read the present burst of enthusiasm for humanitarian interventions merely as a result of the end of the cold war. It is also the manifestation of a kind of idealism (in the nonpejorative sense) that has entered international law and (primarily via international and nongovernmental organizations) the modern international political scene.[2]

The expanding array of human rights commitments at the international level in the aftermath of World War II (perhaps best captured in the post-Holocaust motto, "Never Again") created a legal framework and on-paper commitments by states to prevent gross violations of human rights. Much of the current confusion of American foreign policy in these areas is the result of the fact that this humanitarian law was never well integrated with the older and more-established state sovereignty law. While committed in principle to universal humanitarian standards, the fact remains that any enforcement of those standards depends almost entirely on the voluntary efforts of sovereign states. Understandably, sovereign states are slow to commit blood and money to causes, no matter how noble, that are not demonstrably connected to vital national interests.

Further, the balance of power and proxy wars of the superpowers in the cold war served to assure that only very rarely would a humanitarian crisis be far enough from superpower rivalry for the humanitarian impulse to be played out. Inevitably, claims to humanitarian concern as a basis for intervention would appear (and usually were) a kind of smokescreen behind which the major states jockeyed for position. Equally inevitably, even the most well intentioned efforts at humanitarian intervention would almost always have secondary effects on perceived interests of the superpowers.

The result of this combination of humanitarian legal development and superpower stalemate was that true humanitarian intervention was rare, and the body of law that justified it in theory had little opportunity to generate precedents in practice and little practical need to be better reconciled with state sovereignty law.

The success at coalition building in the Gulf War at the very time of the end of the cold war led President Bush to imagine a "new world order." This would be an order, presumably, of united international support for universal values, and would be led by the United States, under the legal auspices of the United Nations.

It fell to the Clinton administration to spell out the place of humanitarian interventions in the national military strategy of the United States in that new order. The first detailed articulation came in May 1994. Presidential Decision Directive #25 (PDD-25) was entitled *The Clinton Administration's Policy on Reforming Multilateral Peace Operations*. The directive noted that the cold war had severely hampered the ability of the United Nations to do peace operations, but it went on to say: "In the new strategic environment such operations can serve more often as a cost-effective tool to advance American as well as collective interests in maintaining peace in key regions and create global burden-sharing for peace."[3] At this juncture, I would simply note the ambiguity of linking peace operations to "American as well as collective interests" as if they were a single thing. Further, the term "collective" is itself ambiguous. Does it mean NATO? The UN? Coalitions of the willing that shift from crisis to crisis?

PDD-25 proceeded to lay out a number of criteria for US participation in multilateral peace operations and to suggest internal reforms to the UN necessary for future operations to be more professionally planned and executed from a military point of view. It noted that, as presently structured, the UN lacks competent command and control for complex military operations—not to mention common standards of training, interoperability of equipment, and so on.

In May 1997, PDD-56, *"White Paper: The Clinton Administration's Policy on Managing Complex Contingency Operations"* was released.[4] The background statement of this document begins:

> In the wake of the Cold War, attention has focused on a rising number of territorial disputes, armed ethnic conflicts, and civil wars that pose a threat to regional and international peace and may be accompanied by natural or manmade disasters which precipitate massive human suffering. We have learned that effective responses to these situations may require multi-dimensional operations composed of such components as political, diplomatic, humanitarian, intelligence, economic development, and security; hence the term complex contingency operations.[5]

As examples of such operations, the directive cited Haiti, Somalia, northern Iraq and the former Yugoslavia. The primary intent of the directive was to institutionalize lessons learned from those operations to better coordinate various US government agencies in future operations. But it also noted that, very often, such contingency operations take place in complex coalitions as well, "either under the auspices of an international or regional organization or in ad hoc, temporary coalitions of like-minded states."[6]

This framing of international relations in terms of humanitarian interventions in the name of universal principles is not uniquely an

American impulse. UN Secretary General Annan has repeatedly articulated his understanding of the central challenge of the international community in this generation. In his annual report to the General Assembly for 1999, he said, "[T]he core challenge to the Security Council and to the United Nations as a whole in the next century [is] to forge unity behind the principle that massive and systematic violations of human rights—wherever they take place—should not be allowed to stand."[7]

Annan correctly identifies the main obstacle to such an interventionist imperative: not so much the idea of state sovereignty per se, but rather "the ways in which the Member States of the United Nations define their national interest in any given crisis."[8] As he says,

> A new, more broadly defined, more widely conceived definition of national interest in the new century would, I am convinced, induce States to find far greater unity in the pursuit of such basic Charter values as democracy, pluralism, human rights, and the rule of law.[9]

Annan's vision of an effective, consistent, and universal global commitment to the protection of human individuals and their rights appeals to the deepest idealist impulses in all thoughtful people. The Clinton administration policies attempted to go a long way in Annan's direction, while still operating with a less broadly conceived understanding of national interest than Annan's. But differing conceptions of national interest and the fact that Annan's universalizing vision must be accomplished with the forces of sovereign states together generate the competing imperative for US participation in peacekeeping and peacemaking operations: the imperative of force protection. This imperative arises not merely from political constraints, but also from the moral contract between the nation, its citizens, and its military personnel.

The Force Protection Imperative

The dilemma of humanitarian intervention arises from some elementary facts. The "international community" has no army. The United Nations lacks an air force or navy. As Annan states the problem, "Unless the United Nations is given the means and support to succeed, not only the peace, but the war, too, will be lost."[10] But what would it mean to "give the means" to the UN?

One possibility is, of course, to give the UN its own organic military command structure and force structure. If ever universal, consistent, and prompt peace enforcement is to become the international norm, this is the direction in which we would have to move. But equally clearly, there is no political consensus in favor of that development, either in the United States or in the world generally. At most, PDD-25 calls for a strengthening of the UN's capabilities to exercise effective command and control over complex operations by the creation of a small standing military staff, a rapidly deployable headquarters, and prenegotiated contracts for airlift capability, among other things.[11]

Even though the Clinton administration went further than any previous American administration in linking American strategy to participation in multinational operations, PDD-25 went on to say,

> The President retains and will never relinquish command authority over United States forces. On a case by case basis, the President will consider placing appropriate United States forces under the operational control of a competent UN commander for specific UN operations authorized by the Security Council. The greater the United States military role, the less likely it will be that the United States will agree to have a UN commander exercise overall operational control over United States forces. Any large scale participation of United States forces in a major peace enforcement mission that is likely to involve combat should ordinarily be conducted under United States command and operational control or through competent regional organizations such as NATO or ad hoc coalitions.[12]

While this paragraph derives from US policy documents, there can be little doubt that other sovereign states will and must think similar thoughts about putting their military personnel in harm's way.

Partly, this reluctance comes from a distrust of the competence and training level of commanders from other nations—even nations, like those in NATO, with which the United States has worked and trained for fifty years. But if that were the only objection, it could (in theory) be addressed by building up a professional officer corps, organic to the UN, and through frequent joint military exercises under UN command and control. Further, as I indicated above, PDD-25 calls for the development of just such a core competency in the UN itself, and it is a kind of capability Secretary General Annan would clearly welcome.

But there is a larger moral question behind this jurisdictional and political struggle. It goes much deeper than practical questions about the ability of the UN to exercise competent and effective command and control over multinational forces. It also goes deeper than the long-standing tension between state sovereignty and effective international organization. At its root, it goes to the implicit moral contract between the nation and its soldiers. For the sake of specificity, I will not deal with the general case of this question, but specifically with the American case: what is the "deal" implicitly made between America's all-volunteer professional military and national command authorities?

Joining an all-volunteer military such as the contemporary American one may usefully be construed as a kind of "contract." There is, of course, the literal and legal contract, the stuff of recruiting, in which pay is stipulated and educational benefits are spelled out. But I mean to focus more on the implicit moral contract—the kind of "contract" that social contract theories of the state such as those of Hobbes, Locke, and Rawls imagine.

Like those social contracts, the contract is constructed rather than literal. That is to say, just as there never was a real group of human beings in John Rawls's "original position," so there never was a moment when the political leadership of the United States convened a meeting with a group of soldiers and explained the terms of their relationship. But military service is, morally viewed, something more than a career choice.

Military personnel live in a unique moral world. They exist to serve the state. The essence and moral core of their service is to defend that state through the management and application of violence in defense of the territorial integrity, political sovereignty, and vital national interests of that state. Their contract has an "unlimited liability" clause—they accept (and in an all-volunteer force, unquestionably voluntarily accept) the obligation to put their lives and bodies at grave risk when ordered to do so. Their contract also requires them to kill other human beings and to destroy their property when given legal orders to do so.

The unlimited liability clause and the voluntary consent to kill and destroy make the soldier's contract a morally weighty one. No rational person would enter such a contract without morally serious reasons for doing so. While it is true one can be killed or cause the death of others in many other lines of work, in no other profession are they integral to the enterprise itself. At every moment, the soldier's contract puts him or her at risk, if military power is misused, of committing murder or of being maimed or killed in vain. Only if the soldier, sailor, or airman is confident that political authority will only call on military services for morally legitimate and weighty causes can the contract be entered into with confidence and moral security.

One might say, of course, that a military person's obligation is much simpler than this. All that is required is that he or she follows all legal orders. Political leaders, one might say, make the determination to use the military for whatever purposes they deem worthwhile and, so long as the orders are legal, those decisions are "above the pay grade" of the military person.

Legally, this view is, of course, correct. But the legalist answer is the superficial answer. The military contract obliges military personnel to run grave risks and to engage in morally and personally difficult actions. They do these things on the basis of the implicit promise that the circumstances under which they must do so are based on political leadership's good-faith judgment that the defense of the sovereignty and integrity of the nation (or, by careful extension, the nation's vital interests) require their action. The further a particular engagement or deployment departs from this clear "contractual" case, the more difficult it is for political leadership to offer moral and political justification for any killing and especially dying their forces experience.

The imperative for force protection when we use our forces in humanitarian interventions, peacekeeping, and peacemaking operations is, of course, to a large degree political. It is difficult to maintain political support of operations, no matter how well intended, as the casualties mount and the body bags appear on the news. But this "political" problem has a deep moral root in the soldier's contract.

American military personnel are just that—*American* military personnel. The contract they accepted justifies, including to themselves, their violent actions and the risks they accept in the name of serving that state.

When we use those forces for humanitarian causes distantly related to the terms of the contract, they (and their fellow citizens) may accept those deployments in the name of ideals of "international community"—but only up to a certain (and pretty low) threshold of pain. The imperative for force protection in such deployment is only superficially some aversion to casualties induced by Vietnam syndrome. At a deeper level it goes to the core of the moral meaning of military service to a sovereign state.[13] To such a use of American forces, the military person may say with moral seriousness, "This isn't what I signed up for"—and all the more if casualties mount, the length of the deployment drags on, and the probability of achieving the goal of the mission declines.

Kofi Annan is correct when he suggests that building an effective international consensus to use military force consistently for humanitarian purposes would require a broader construal of "national interest" than has classically been the case. As PDD-25 argued, it would require considerable attention to internal UN mechanisms to command and control such operations. There are far too many legitimate moral reactions to world events that boil down to "somebody should do something about that." But is the response to be an effective and universal application of political and, if necessary, military power of the international community? If so, such a program would require extensive and concentrated international attention for many years to put political and military structures in place that could begin to meet the need.

The interim use of American forces for purposes tangentially and marginally connected to defense and the national interest will be filled with compromises. Even if the UN or other agencies of the "international community" could find the political and moral will to authorize such interventions consistently and according to uniform moral and political standards of judgment, such deployments would be problematic.

There will inevitably be more missions than willing forces. The political will to support use of national forces for them will be unreliable and easily dissipated. These political realities are grounded in the deeper moral issue of the contract implicitly made between the nation and its military. A consequence of this moral (and political) reality is that national forces will be used inconsistently in the full spectrum of peace operations, and that force protection will be among the highest priorities when they are so used.

Perhaps "national interest" will come to be defined as broadly as Kofi Annan advocates. The American public would need, of course, to embrace that redefinition with enthusiasm for it to work—and be prepared to sacrifice significant blood and money in the pursuit of national interest, so defined. Or perhaps over time international organizations will be strengthened enough to deploy in such circumstances.

But until that happens, humanitarian intervention and peace operations will be piecemeal, inconsistent, and dependent on coalitions of the willing. They will be (and, morally, need to be) risk-averse, and highly focused on force protection.

Protection of innocent foreign nationals will be a priority as well—for the political reason that any injuring and killing of civilians obviously undermine the moral basis of humanitarian intervention, but also because of the moral concern with protection of innocent life. But even the concern with protection of innocents will probably be secondary to force protection of our own troops, for the weighty moral reasons we have explored here.

Can humanitarian interventions be supported and successfully executed under such constraints? The best answer we have at the moment is, I fear, "occasionally." Traditional just war thinking places a high premium on the lives of innocents in conflict, and requires combatants to take measures, even at risk to themselves, to protect those lives. But in an operation such as Kosovo, where the moral basis of significant risk of loss by our own soldiers was questionable, there was a significant (and potentially troubling) change to that traditional calculus. Gen. Wesley Clark has written clearly about this:

> The minimization of civilian casualties and damage to civilian structures and property—whether Serb or Kosovar—was very high on our priority list. Any lack of discrimination between legitimate military targets and off-limits civilian areas would

have undercut our efforts to explain what we were doing and maintain public support.[14]

There can be no doubt that NATO's bombing campaign in Kosovo and Serbia strove mightily to meet this requirement. Even more than in the Gulf War the weapons employed were precise, both because of technical improvements since the Gulf War and because an even higher percentage of all weapons used were precision munitions. Over 23,000 bombs and missiles were expended in this campaign, and a record 35 percent of them were smart weapons.[15]

Despite this emphasis on precision in an air campaign conducted at about 15,000 feet, one cannot help but note that the precision would have been higher still had the aircraft operated at lower altitudes (and greater risk). Further, the decision to adopt and announce in advance an airpower-only campaign certainly lengthened the conflict and ensured that very little would be done in Kosovo to bring to a halt the atrocities that were the cause of the campaign itself. Since those small and dispersed units on the ground were not very susceptible to effective targeting, given the chosen weapons platforms and tactics NATO implicitly embarked on a war of attrition against Serbian infrastructure. No matter how precise the weapons employed, widespread destruction of national infrastructure is inherently an indiscriminate attack on the whole population.

Here we see the deep issue for further thought. No matter how idealistic the motives for humanitarian interventions, force-protection considerations may restrict the means to the point that the operation is unlikely to halt the atrocities in question and will have the foreseeable effect of widespread misery for innocent civilians. And if that is so, one must reassess the moral equation at the basis of the intervention. It is worth thinking about what would have happened had Serbia not capitulated when it did. How widely would we have let the target list expand? How far were we really prepared to go in destroying the Serbian economy, power grid, transportation system, and so forth, in the name of "precision" air war?

Even humanitarian military operations are subject to one of the crucial tests of just war: reasonable hope of success. Most dangerous of all is the impulse to intervene, but to do so with such restraint and caution that one merely adds damage to an already bad situation. Such interventions may indeed have no reasonable hope of success in solving the problem that caused the intervention in the first place.

Kosovo points to the deep need to rethink the moral contract between soldiers and their society. We need to consider in hard, practical terms the connection of the means we are willing to use and the political and military ends we seek. Only if we can and do bring effective means to bear on those ends, within the constraints of the morally acceptable, can future humanitarian operations fulfill the requirement of reasonable hope of success.

Eight

Strategic Theory, Military Practice, and the Laws of War: The Case of Strategic Bombing

From its origins, air war has been subject to a peculiarly and dramatically bifurcated way of thinking. With its ability to leap across borders and attack virtually anywhere, airpower has threatened to destroy the last vestiges of just war's effort to keep noncombatants immune from direct and deliberate attack.

The combatant/noncombatant distinction had been under pressure from the industrialization of war for some time before airpower's advent, but the prospect of air war's deliberate attack on urban centers seemed likely to render it permanently moot. On the brighter side, airpower offered the possibility of breaking out of the stagnant wars of attrition and defensive lines of World War I. Direct attack on enemy vital centers promised a new era of humane war that would target directly the industrial and logistical support of the war effort, and only secondarily human beings, whether in or out of uniform.

Early enthusiasts of airpower also suggested it would enormously reduce the length of war by quickly destroying the economic and industrial bases necessary to sustain conflict.

As the use of airpower evolved through World War II and beyond, it began to appear that the prophecy of the obliteration of the combatant/noncombatant distinction would be fulfilled, while precision targeting of vital centers would remain an empty ideal. However the targeting strategy for nuclear weapons in the cold war varied, it seemed increasingly clear that the moral restraints on war that lay at the core of the just war tradition were archaic. Some shreds of just war thinking might remain in the law books, and occasionally its constraints might be implemented in small-scale wars such as the Falklands conflict. For direct conflict between the United States and the Soviet Union, however, the probability that war would be conducted within meaningful restraints of the just war was essentially nil. It did not require a subtle mind to determine that a full-scale conventional war between NATO and the Warsaw Pact would, in any credible scenario, inevitably evolve into at least a theaterwide total war with nuclear weapons. Almost equally certainly, it would cascade to global total war. In either case, noncombatant immunity would, to put it mildly, certainly not be respected.

This was true most especially, perhaps, in regard to air war. Strategic bombing would inevitably lead to bombing of targets in major population centers. Such bombing would, either by design or by accident (due to the limitations of the targeting mechanisms and weaponry available) be tantamount to World War II style area bombing. Whatever the claims, bombing would inevitably involve huge numbers of direct civilian deaths due to inaccurate weapons and navigation.

The uses of airpower in the Gulf Wars and in the Kosovo bombing campaign, however, challenge this apparently inevitable historical progression. In those conflicts, vast applications of airpower produced very little destruction of civilian life and property (leaving aside for the moment targets bombed with precision, but in error), even in the bombing of targets in highly urbanized environments. For the first time in the history of airpower, it looked as though the promise of precision strategic bombing might, at last, be fulfilled.

Of course there were many characteristics of the Gulf Wars that give us pause in drawing too sweeping conclusions about the future of air war generally for they may have been unique.

The desert environment in which frontline troops met allowed the use of inherently indiscriminant weapons such as "dumb bombs" (the vast majority of the weapons discharged in the First Gulf War) without endangering civilian lives. Further, the total air supremacy of Coalition forces in the theater was an element that may not be assumed in future conflicts. Nevertheless, the new technologies of the F-117, cruise missile, and various kinds of precision munitions made a dramatic debut in the Gulf War,[1] and they presage whole new classes of precision weapons in future air war.

The Kosovo campaign marked yet a further evolution, both in technology and in strategy. On the one hand, the weapons systems employed were a generation beyond those in the Gulf War. For example, the difficulties with laser-designators as guidance systems—they are easily confused by dust and smoke—were largely overcome by the use of satellite signals from the global positioning system to direct weapons to their targets. The B-2 bomber made its combat debut, making possible far larger precision strikes by stealth platforms than the F-117 was capable of delivering.

The new air weapons do tempt political leaders to employ "air only" campaigns of dubious strategic value.[2] The downside of the Gulf War's precision, especially on the *jus ad bellum* dimension of just war theory, was made abundantly clear by the decisions regarding how to use precision airpower in the Kosovo campaign. In that campaign the very precision of airpower, coupled with the impunity given by stealth and standoff weapons capability, served dramatically to lower the threshold for the use of military force.

Still, the emergence of precision weapons and new tactics for their use marks a distinctive turn in the attempt to assimilate air war to the laws and moral principles of just war. It strengthens the prospect of at last bringing air war under the umbrella of the central moral principles of just war and it also points to novel areas for moral reflection on the use of such new weapons.[3] Before turning to these novel considerations, however, let us set their historical context.

From its very beginning, airpower has been as much the subject of fantasy as of careful rational thought about its military potential. As Michael Sherry observed in *The Rise of American Airpower*,

> Never viewed solely as a weapon, the airplane was the instrument of flight, of a whole new dimension in human activity. Therefore it was uniquely capable of stimulating fantasies of peacetime possibilities for lifting worldly burdens, transforming man's sense of time and space, transcending geography, knitting together nations and peoples, releasing humankind from its biological limits."[4]

Soon after the airplane's invention, the laws of war rushed to accommodate and attempted to regulate the new possibilities for the conduct of war the airplane made possible. In the Hague Conference of 1907, prohibition was made of "bombardment, by whatever means" of "undefended" cities.[5] Such efforts seem quaint, given the subsequent history of the use of airpower. But it is important to note that as early as this there was the recognition that the indiscriminate attacks on cities made possible by aerial bombardment would be legally and morally unacceptable. Further, the Hague Conference recognized that such attacks, if they ever were to be accepted as means of legitimate warfare, would obliterate the prohibition on the deliberate attack on civilians that lay at the heart of just war restrictions.

Speculation about the practical military uses of airpower consistently traded on the ambiguity of two quite different targeting ideas. On the one hand, early theorists such as Billy Mitchell envisioned the strategic use of airpower to attack the "vital centers" of an enemy, thereby avoiding the need to confront line armies in the field.[6] Ideal targets would be those essential facilities of production of war materiel, and of command, control and communication, that made it possible to sustain a fighting force in the field. On the other hand, airpower made it possible to entertain the possibility of direct strikes at enemy civilian populations in hope of sapping the will to fight.

This course was explicitly laid out and advocated by the Italian theorist Douhet in his highly influential 1921 book, *The Command of the Air*. Douhet's idea was not that airpower should destroy targets of direct and demonstrable relation to the capabilities of fielded military forces. Instead, direct wholesale bombing of urban populations would serve to end war quickly, not so much because of the physical destruction of the enemy's weapons and communications systems but more because it would lead to the collapse of the civil society that sustained and fielded those forces. As Douhet wrote, "How could a country go on living and working under this constant threat, oppressed by the nightmare of imminent destruction and death? How indeed!"[7] The efficacy of such attacks was, apparently, deemed to be so obvious that further argument was unnecessary.

When Douhet-inspired thinkers such as Britain's Trenchard wrote to address the moral justification of such a plan of attack, they were, of course, aware that intentionally bombing civilian

populations would obliterate the noncombatant immunity principle. Thus, with tortured logic Trenchard insisted that bombing of
whole urban areas was not "for the sole purpose of terrorising the
civilian population" but had a legitimate military purpose in bombing "to terrorise [sic] munitions workers (men and women) into
absenting themselves from work."[8] The very illogic of such a "distinction" bears tribute to the strongly felt need to find a moral
defense for the plan.

One can see the haziness in strategic thinking, and the conse-
quent confusion about the most efficacious (never mind morally
preferable) use of strategic bombing. On one interpretation, the
purpose of strategic bombing is to destroy specific identifiable targets. These targets are selected because intelligence indicates that
they are the sources of production or distribution of specific items
essential to the conduct of military operations or are the crucial
points of command, control, intelligence coordination, or other
important military functions. On the other, however, so-called
strategic bombing is really a euphemism for deliberate attacks on
populated areas with the intent of demoralizing the population.
The rationale for this mode of attack is the belief that the conse-
quent demoralization and disorientation of the civilian population
will force enemy political and military leadership to capitulate. Of
course, the limited accuracy of bombardment through the Second
World War made the distinction largely moot. Still, it remained an
important conceptual distinction, and one that would have practical consequence as the technology of air war evolved.

Although too complex to rehearse in detail here, in many
ways the history of the use of airpower in World War II can be
mapped as a complex interplay between these two distinct, yet
often blurred fundamental ideas. The differing opinions of the
British and American air arms regarding the preferred method of
bombing Germany early in the war play out this doctrinal dispute.
American doctrine argued for "precision daylight" bombing. Partly
as a consequence of the repugnance to wholesale terror bombing,
and partly because it believed it would be more militarily effective, American theorists argued for careful targeting of key nodes
in the enemy's economic and military system. Sherry writes,
"[Precision bombing] promised victory independent of the other
branches of the armed forces, with minimal demands on and risks

for Americans, employing the bomber as an instrument of surgical precision rather than indiscriminate horror, laying its high explosives (not gas or incendiaries) on its targets with pinpoint accuracy, incapacitating the enemy without slaughter."[9]

In contrast, the British advocated forthrightly bombing of built-up areas for the purpose of terrorization, believing this would cause German society to collapse and quickly end the war.

Despite these theoretical differences, in practice American technology was only slightly more able than British to deliver on the promise of precision bombing for the whole of the war. This became even more the case as German air defense improved and forced the bombers to higher altitudes for their bombing. American and British decision-makers, perceiving the need to show some means of bringing home the war, first to the German and then to the Japanese public, pushed the military in the direction of terror bombing. These factors made area bombing the actual practice of the Allied air forces throughout the war.[10]

Indeed, by the end of the war American bombing was directed away from strategic operations such as mine laying in the sealanes (which might well have had a direct impact on the enemy's ability to wage war) in favor of a policy of incendiary bombing of Japanese cites.[11]

But for bombing in urban areas, to repeat the point, the debate regarding pinpoint versus area bombing was pretty much a distinction without a difference. Close analysis of the effect of a hundred air raids into Germany revealed that even in 1941 "not one bomb in three had hit within five miles of its designated target, and there were extreme errors of up to a hundred miles."[12] Given these realities, area bombing was the reality, regardless of the intent.

The historical record of World War II is well known and well documented, and for our purposes here does not require rehearsing in detail. What is clear is that it was not technically feasible to engage in pinpoint strategic bombing, given the technology available at the time. But neither was it generally deemed desirable to refrain from area bombing or to attempt to restrict civilian deaths to the category of reasonable collateral damage within the framework of such a careful bombing campaign.

It is only with the wisdom of hindsight that after World War II US Air Force doctrine on this point became clearer. Until quite recently, air force doctrine identified "two basic target sets" for strategic bombing: "those that would affect enemy capability to conduct military operations and those that would affect enemy will to continue fighting."[13] Even this formulation, of course, begs the question of which targets might affect "enemy will"—targets that demoralize combatants, or direct attacks on civilian populations?

After World War II it was increasingly apparent that the use of area bombing campaigns with the intent to terrorize civilian populations and demoralize enemy citizens was a dubious use of military resources. Compared to attack on targets that directly affected the enemy's capability to conduct military operations, it was almost always ineffective.

Although recognized in theory, this realization had little opportunity for large scale testing in Korea and Vietnam, where much of the use of airpower was the air support to ground troops rather than the engagement of strategic targets. When strategic bombing was attempted, the inaccuracy of weapons made the pinpoint targets notoriously difficult to destroy at least until laser-guided munitions became available toward the end of the Vietnam War. Further, when strategic bombing was conducted in Vietnam in the Linebacker II operation, even though exclusively military targets were selected, collateral damage was extensive. This damage was due partly to the inaccuracy of unguided munitions dropped from B-52s and partly to Vietnamese air defense weapons that, having missed their targets, returned to earth and exploded.

In this period, thinking about truly strategic air war was relegated to the planning of the use of nuclear weapons. Even in nuclear planning, however, the counterforce versus countervalue targeting debate and issues of the prudence of thinking about "winnable" nuclear war failed to truly help the discussion. And needless to say, the enormous destructive force of the weapons themselves made it difficult to distinguish pinpoint from area bombing in practice, regardless of the targeting theory.

Only in the Gulf and Kosovo wars did technology, political circumstance, and the nature of the enemy social organization combine to provide a new "experiment" in the efficacy of pinpoint strategic bombing. In its aftermath it is apparent that air war has entered a genuinely new phase in its history. The experience of the First Gulf War suggested that the prophecies of early air war visionaries might finally be fulfilled to a large degree. Still the very success of the air campaign points to new issues for exploration in the ongoing dialogue on international law and the law of nations regarding just conduct in war.

In 1922-23, legal experts convened at The Hague to draft rules for air war that would, at a minimum, prohibit avoidable killing of civilians. Although these rules were never ratified by any state, many air forces did incorporate the gist of these rules into operational manuals,[14] and leaders still spoke of using airpower within the restraints of the Just War. For example, in 1938, in an address to the House of Commons, the British prime minister said,

> In the first place, it is against international law to make deliberate attacks upon civilian populations. In the second place, targets that are aimed at from the air must be legitimate military objects and must be capable of identification. In the third place, reasonable care must be taken in attacking those military objects so that by carelessness a civilian population in the neighbourhood is not bombed.[15]

Despite this appearance of agreement prior to World War II, the war evolved a style of air war in which all pretense of maintaining this moral line was erased. Deliberate "area" or "carpet" bombing of cities became the standard practice, especially for the Allies. Partly, this was a result of technological and operational constraints on the aircraft, targeting, and navigation systems available at the time. It was also a result of an explicit attempt to make civilian morale a direct object of attack; in addition, it was an emotionally driven response to the German use of grossly indiscriminate weapons such as the V-1 and V-2 rockets.

This common practice did not in any way alter the legal understanding that direct attacks on civilian populations were prohibited. At the close of the war, the Nuremberg Tribunals were chartered to consider "wanton destruction of cities, towns, and villages, or devastation not justified by military necessity."[16] Nuremberg declined to prosecute cases involving air war on the part of Axis powers, at least partially in recognition that Allied practice would be subject to precisely the same strictures.

The major shift in international law on this point is marked by the passage of Additional Protocol I to the Geneva Convention in 1977. Although unratified by the United States and most other major powers, it nonetheless establishes a binding understanding of the customary law of war in the minds of United States military officials.[17] Additional Protocol I, Article 48, clearly codifies what (arguably) had been unclearly stated previously: "The basic rule requires that a distinction must be made at all times between the civilian population and combatants and between civilian objects and military objectives, and that operations must accordingly be directed only against military objectives."[18]

Further, the protocol states that attackers must take "every precaution" to minimize incidental civilian losses and to ensure that such losses or damage not be excessive in relation to the concrete and direct military advantage sought.[19]

In his comprehensive review of international law as it bears on air war, W. Hayes Parks writes,

Article 48 states the fundamental principle of discrimination, a principle on which there should be no disagreement. Indeed, military efficiency calls for discrimination to the extent that it is reasonably possible, and the United States historically has used its technological superiority to endeavor to gain increased accuracy in order to be as discriminate as possible in placing munitions on the target.[20]

However one judges the morality and legality of the kind of air war the Allies conducted in World War II,[21] a similar pattern of targeting and target selection would clearly be illegal in the contemporary context. This is codified as official Air Force interpretation of international law. After reviewing the conduct of air operations in World War II, United States Air Force interpretation of the laws of war states, "The civilian population as such, as well as individual civilians shall not be made the object of attack. Acts or threats of violence which have the primary object of spreading terror among the civilian population are prohibited."[22]

This understanding of international law dovetails nicely with an improved understanding of the militarily efficacious uses of airpower. Further, technological developments reviewed above now permit the application of airpower in ways largely congruent with such principles.[23]

Understandings of international law regarding armed conflict have practical force only insofar as they are incorporated in the doctrinal statements, the operational planning and training, and even the weapons acquisition pattern of the armed forces of nations. Only insofar as military forces incorporate those legal principles into the routines of "how we do business" do they have real action-guiding force. It is appropriate, therefore, to survey the official articulations of doctrine and theory regarding the application of airpower in contemporary United States Air Force thinking.

The most influential thinker regarding strategic bombing in the contemporary US Air Force is John A. Warden III. His book, *The Air Campaign: Planning for Combat*, has been incorporated into the teaching at the United States Air Force Academy and at the various professional schools officers attend as they advance through the ranks. To a great extent, the air campaign executed in the First Gulf War was the product of Warden's theories, and was actually planned by his close associates. Author Rick Atkinson wrote in *Crusade*, his history of the Gulf War, "In war no less than in peace, success has a thousand fathers, and paternity claims in the Persian Gulf War would mount in direct proportion to allied achievements. Yet no claim is stronger than Warden's."[24]

Warden's book begins with the assertion that planning for effective air war has been hampered by the lack of coherent thinking about the operational level of war planning. By "operational" Warden means the middle level, lying between the grand strategic plan for the overall conduct of the war and the tactical level, which concerns the achievement of reasonably discrete and identifiable objectives in battle. The operational level "is primarily concerned with how to achieve the strategic ends of the war with the forces allotted," and is generally the concern of the theater commander (rather than, say, of the Joint Chiefs of Staff).[25] In short, Warden's theory purports to guide the theater planner in finding the right fit between the overall goals of the war, on the one hand, and the panoply of resources available in theater for accomplishing those goals.

Warden argues strenuously that the air force has historically been crippled by an excessively narrow, "tactical," kind of thinking about the proper application of airpower. Modern weapons make possible long dreamed-of direct attack on enemy "centers of gravity."[26] This requires more careful thought about the operational level of planning.

Warden schematizes his theory in terms of five concentric circles, representing the five "centers of gravity" in an enemy state. The central and smallest circle represents enemy leadership. The second represents infrastructure and supplies essential to military operations, such as petroleum and electrical power. The third includes other elements of infrastructure such as transportation. Fourth is the enemy population, and fifth the fielded military forces of the enemy. In a dramatic statement of his theory, Warden writes, "Strategic warfare is only indirectly concerned with what is happening on some distant battlefield"; instead, it should aim at vital centers usually far behind the lines.[27]

Warden's theoretical ideas, articulated in *The Air Campaign*, received their baptism by fire in the air campaign in Desert Storm. Although Warden's strategic campaign plan was initially dismissed by senior officers as the raving of an "airpower airhead" its essential framework survived in the plan for opening phase of the Desert Storm air campaign.[28]

Warden's views have progressively been reflected in official US Air Force doctrinal statements.[29] Regarding strategic targeting, for example, official air force guidance from 1992 stated: "In large measure, successful strategic attack operations depend on proper identification of the enemy's major vulnerabilities—centers of gravity. Against a modern industrialized opponent . . . a center of gravity may be discerned by a careful analysis of the enemy's industrial infrastructure, logistics system, population centers, and command and control apparatus."[30]

Further, it noted "The capability to put any asset an enemy possesses at extreme risk, at any time, largely fulfills the theory of strategic airpower expressed by aviation's pioneers and visionaries."[31]

Unfortunately, neither Warden's work nor air force manuals of the 1990's were as clear on the issue of deliberate targeting of civilians as one would wish, or as international law would require. Warden, for example, writes, "The theater commander should consider all kinds of operations that might have an influence on the campaign. If the will of the enemy people is vulnerable, the theater commander may want to concentrate efforts against that target."[32]

Similarly, Air Force Manual 1-1, volume II (superceded only in 1998) said:

> A basic premise of early airpower theorists was that political and industrial targets deep behind enemy lines presented the most vulnerable and lucrative areas for attack and provided the greatest leverage for a favorable outcome to a war. The advent of airpower made possible direct strikes against such targets, thus presenting the prospect of ending a conflict quickly by destroying an enemy's ability to wage war or by convincing him to desist without first having to fight and defeat his military forces. In the development of these theories, two basic target sets emerged: those that would affect enemy capability to conduct military operations and those that would affect enemy will to continue fighting.[33]

On the issue of deliberate attack on enemy civilian morale, however, the 1992 manual commented only weakly and with understatement "[S]trategic attack has rarely affected enemy morale to the degree anticipated by early airpower enthusiasts."[34] Only buried in a footnote do we find the more precise statement:

> Early airpower theorists assumed that civilian populations would be more vulnerable and susceptible to the psychological impact of massed airpower than would military personnel in combat. Ironically, history appears to demonstrate that civilian resistance tends to stiffen under persistent strategic air attacks . . ."[35]

Later doctrine of the United States Air Force advanced the discussion to a degree. Air Force Doctrine Document 2-1.2, "Strategic Attack," (20 May, 1998) stated,

> The historic focus of classic US strategic attack theory since its development in the 1930s has been on the war-making capacity and will of the enemy. Today, while these traditional goals

and sequential attack techniques may still have relevance during prolonged major conflicts, the advent of precision munitions, stealth technology, advanced information warfare (IW) techniques, and near-real-time capable command, control and intelligence systems has fostered different possibilities.

For example, one approach involves the parallel, rather than sequential, attack of a series of targets. The goal is to cripple the enemy's national political and military leadership's ability to act and bring elements of the national infrastructure and, resources permitting, operational and tactical targets under attack. Through overwhelming parallel attack of critical centers, the enemy's strategy is defeated by reducing or removing its capability to conduct military operations. No longer must air forces serially destroy each target class before moving on to the next.[36]

The emphasis in contemporary Air Force thinking is on "centers of gravity" (defined as "those characteristics, capabilities, or localities from which a military force, nation, or alliance derives its freedom of action, physical strength, or will to fight."[37]). It is not the total destruction of a set of targets that matters, so contemporary Air Force doctrine opines, but the "synergistic effect" of a swift attack on the "system of systems" upon which the enemy depends for situational awareness and coordinated defense and attack. Strategic planning informed by this view is "effects based," attempting to achieve clear disruption of enemy capability rather than large-scale physical destruction of property.

Furthermore, current air force doctrine goes farther than previous versions in acknowledging the wishful thinking of some previously articulated understandings of the working of airpower: "The process of linking ends and means is a critical requirement for the air strategist. The ultimate results are often psychological in nature; war is after all a human endeavor, and attempting to predict human reaction too precisely can be difficult. Nevertheless, understanding the links between cause and either physical or psychological effect is a key part of air warfare planning. *Failure to properly analyze the mechanism that ties tactical results to strategic effects has historically been the shortcoming of both airpower theorists and strategists.*"[38]

The First Gulf War "Lessons Learned"

Despite the somewhat cloudy statements of doctrine at the time, in practice planners of the air campaigns in the Gulf and Kosovo wars were careful in target selection to minimize civilian casualties. They avoided any hint of deliberate targeting of civilians. Further, they were extremely scrupulous about minimizing collateral damage to civilians and civilian objects that might result from targeting of clearly military targets.

Both at the level of political leadership and as implemented at the level of the targeting staff, the language and constraints of just war were extensively employed in the planning of those air campaigns. Legal advisors were assigned to the targeting staff to insure that the bombing campaign conformed to the requirements of international law. Obviously the motives for this were mixed. Among the mix of reasons were a real growth in understanding of the legal and moral constraints required in air war, the availability of weapons of sufficient precision to make constrained conflict possible, and a political concern with public opinion and avoiding adverse press coverage.

However varied the causes, however, the air campaign in the First Gulf War marked a "revolution in warfare."[39] Although very large numbers of weapons were delivered, many in built-up urban areas, for the first time in the history of air war noncombatant injuries and death as a result of direct discharge of weapons were remarkably few. Apart from clear (although serious) mistakes, civilian casualties seem largely to have been proportionate collateral damage, secondary to attacks on legitimate military targets. Furthermore, airpower's long-promised and never-delivered abilities to destroy pinpoint targets and thereby to disable enemy air defense, command, control communications, intelligence, and logistic operations were displayed to a truly remarkable degree.

The study of civilian casualties in Iraq conducted by Middle East Watch, although dramatically titled *Needless Deaths in the Gulf War: Civilian Casualties during the Air Campaign and Violations of the Laws of War*, is very thin in actual cases. Disposed to be highly critical, even this study admits, "[I]n many if not most respects the allies' conduct was consistent with their stated intent to take all feasible precautions to avoid civilian casualties." Indeed, the "violations of the laws of war" they cite rest almost entirely on dubious interpretations of the provisions of Additional Protocol I to the Geneva conventions of 1977. For example, the authors suggest that bombing legitimate military targets in civilian areas should have been conducted exclusively at night, rather than during the day when civilians were more likely to be near them—a nice idea when technically possible, but hardly a requirement of the laws of war. Further, the study cites official Iraqi accounts of large numbers of civilian casualties, but then notes that their own interviews with Iraqi physicians yielded a far lower set of casualty figures. It arrives at the conclusion that, apart from significant loss of life in the single instance of the bombing of the Ameriyya shelter, civilian casualties as a direct result of Coalition bombing were very low.[40]

For the first time in the history of the use of military aviation, there were few or no deaths of civilians due to direct and deliberate targeting of them or of civilian structures. Inherently inaccurate weapons (so-called dumb bombs) were not used in tactical situations where large numbers of civilian deaths were foreseeable and direct civilian deaths were reduced to very low numbers indeed. It is too strong, of course, to claim that the air war in the First Gulf War achieved perfection in bringing air war into conformity with the principles of noncombatant immunity. As the Government Accounting Office evaluation of the air war noted, despite its obvious success, the air war was hampered in its desired effectiveness by a number of factors.[41] Deficiencies of timely bomb damage assessment (BDA) were marked, and such deficiencies necessitated restriking targets. Obviously, restrikes put both civilians and pilots at additional and, in principle, unnecessary risks. Further, an understandable emphasis on pilot and aircraft survivability resulted in delivery of weapons from much higher altitudes than were used in training.[42] Such tactics degraded considerably the accuracy of some weapons, increasing the risk of civilian death. Bad weather, smoke, and the deliberate firing of oil wells by Iraqi forces further degraded the accuracy of weapons that depended on optical sensors or on pilot laser designation of targets. Clearly, these difficulties indicated the need for enhanced sensor capability. Some of those improvements were indeed made in time for the Kosovo campaign.[43] Still, the experience of the First Gulf War and the kind of precision air war it points to an area where further careful thought needs to be given in order to enhance the salutary direction in which air war is evolving in bringing its conduct more squarely within the scope of just war.

The most pressing and difficult problem is the moral status of dual use targets. These are targets whose destruction is reasonably believed to afford a real military advantage, but the destruction of which has clearly foreseeable and significant impact on civilian health, well-being, and perhaps even survival. This problem is by no means unprecedented in the history of air war. But it achieves a much sharper focus in light of the development of weapons, weapons platforms, and tactics after Desert Storm. In the pursuit of the goal of "one bomb, one target"[44] it is foreseeable that in future war there can be less and less direct destruction of civilian life and property as a result of deliberate targeting.[45] This goal is not completely achievable, of course, due to inevitable equipment failures, intelligence failures in target identification, and simple human error. But there can be no question that, from a legal and moral perspective, further development in these directions is to be applauded and pursued.[46]

Even in an imagined "one bomb, one target" environment, with the benefit of perfect intelligence as to the nature of the targets selected, the moral concern to protect civilian life and property to the greatest extent possible points to an area where considerable further analysis is needed. In any reasonably modern society, the parts of the complex web of technical infrastructure necessary to maintain life and health of the population are enormously interdependent. Modern urban life for civilians depends on available clean water, electrical power, sanitation, and garbage removal. Further, in the wartime context, treatment of casualties as well as the routine aspects of civilian health care depend on electrical power for refrigeration of medicines and foodstuffs and for use of technical equipment for health care provision. Even my imagined "perfect" air war might avoid all direct civilian casualties and still, in its destruction of dual use targets, create huge numbers of civilian deaths and injuries — all, of course, of the "bomb now, die later" variety, rather than direct casualties of bombing.

Ramsey Clark's provocative book, *The Fire This Time: United States War Crimes in the Gulf* documents in detail the effects of sanctions on the civilian population of Iraq. Clearly, the deliberate targeting of aspects of the civilian infrastructure, while it does not involve immediate and direct destruction of civilian life, increased the suffering and death toll of the civilian population.[47] Further, it was intended to do so in the hope that Iraq would perceive the need to seek external help to restore infrastructural elements such as electrical power, and be motivated to shorten the war.[48]

To some degree these issues are addressed (at least in principle) under the rubric of proportionality. One assesses the "distinct military advantage offered at the time" (Additional Protocol I, Geneva Convention) of targets in relation to their foreseen effects on civilians. But the concept of proportionality here is highly elastic and imprecise, especially in determination of the relevant span of time within which proportionality is to be assessed.

I do not mean to suggest that morally and legally conscientious targeteers are oblivious to this issue. In the Gulf War, for example, there was a serious effort to take such matters into consideration. *The Gulf War Airpower Survey, Summary Report* writes that in response to written directives of Brig. Gen. Buster C. Glosson,

> Planners wished to minimize long-term damage to Iraq's economic infrastructure, even as they provided for attacks against both electricity and oil targets. This constraint led air planners and targeting specialists to try to restrict attacks on Iraqi electric power to strikes on transformer/switching yards and control buildings rather than on generator halls, boilers, and turbines in order to minimize recuperation time after the conflict ended. Similarly, attacks on oil production were supposed to concentrate on refined-product storage; distillation and other refining areas were to be aimpoints only if they produced military fuels.[49]

For a variety of technical reasons (primarily the inability of pilots to distinguish between the buildings at the plant due to smoke, haze, and the stress of combat), these attempts to restrict targets were ineffective. Attacks on electrical power had the following effects:

> [T]he attacks rapidly shut down the generation and distribution of commercial electric power throughout most of Iraq,

forcing the Iraqi leadership and military on to back-up power. Ultimately, almost eighty-eight percent of Iraq's installed generation capacity was sufficiently damaged or destroyed by direct attack, or else isolated from the national grid through strikes on associated transformers and switching facilities, to render it unavailable. The remaining twelve percent, mainly resident in numerous smaller plants that were not attacked, was probably only available locally because of damage inflicted on transformers and switching yards.[50]

Similar points could be made regarding the destruction of petroleum products, transportation systems, and other dual use targets. "The Harvard Study Team reported sharply increased levels of gastroenteritis, cholera, typhoid, and malnutrition in Iraqi children due to the delayed effects of the Gulf War," largely the loss of electrical power from the bombing.[51] William M. Arkin, then of Greenpeace, estimated 111,000 civilian deaths as a result of the indirect detrimental health effects of the war.[52] These effects occurred despite the fact that the "Iraqis restored commercial power considerably faster then anticipated."[53] Another study claimed "bombing of electrical power 'contributed to' 70,000-90,000 postwar civilian deaths above normal mortality rates over the period April-December 1991, principally because of the lack of electricity in Iraq for water purification and sewage treatment following the cease-fire."[54]

Kosovo

The Kosovo bombing campaign, while it bore many signs of continuity with the Gulf War, was also in many respects quite different. First, the technology had evolved considerably. The difficulties with laser and optical guidance systems the Gulf War had revealed were largely overcome by the development of global positioning system guidance systems for the precision munitions. The first combat use of the B-2's far greater ordinance capacity within a stealth platform greatly enhanced the delivery of precision guided munitions (PGMs) in large quantities.

The political context of the Kosovo campaign, however, did not allow air planners to execute anything like a doctrinally correct air campaign. The fragility of the NATO coalition and political consid-erations arising from the highly debatable legal and moral justifica-tion of the campaign itself forced planners to constrain radically all aspects of the air campaign, from micromanaging target selection to severing entirely the air campaign from its doctrinally mandated connection to the follow-on ground campaign.[55]

The initial phase of the air campaign was highly successful in taking down Serbian air defenses. But the commitment to an "air only" war forced planners farther and farther down the target list, resulting in colossal errors such as the Chinese embassy bombing. That air-only commitment forced ever-widening attacks on Serbian infrastructure—in effect, making the will of the civilian population and its political support of the regime once again the target. Fortunately, the campaign ended when it did. Had it continued much longer, the "bomb now, die later" consequences to the civil-ian population would quickly have been dire.

Further, the mismatch between the dispersed Serbian ground forces conducting the ethnic cleansing in Kosovo and the high-alti-tude fast fighters committed to the mission made airpower seem impotent (as it largely was against that kind of force). There was, and will remain, a dispute over whether it was mere risk aversion that prevented use of the Apache helicopters and other air assets against those ground forces, or whether the inability of any air-power to deal with such a dispersed ground force points to another inherent limit to airpower.

What Kosovo reveals most graphically is that precision deliv-ery of munitions has very real limits. Timothy J. Sakulich has cap-tured the problem perfectly in saying, "...the causal relationship between aerial attacks and political outcomes remains murky."[56] Sakulich further distinguishes "exactness" (precision of the weapon) from "correctness" (matching the attack to the foreseen effect), and points out that the connection between the two is a purely hypothetical.

Of course, some air force thinkers claim the problem is entirely that they were hamstrung and unable to execute the Kosovo air campaign as they would have if left to their own devices. Surely there is some truth in that claim. But Sakulich correctly argues that the problem lies deeper, and has to do with the murky connection between destruction of any given target set and the desired political outcomes of the campaign. In air force jargon, the ability effectively to understand an adversary correctly enough to determine genuine "centers of gravity" remains a challenge.

Conclusions

Airpower is emerging into a new historical phase in terms of its capabilities and limitations. From the perspective of ethics, the news is mostly positive. At least for some conflicts and in some applications, airpower can at last be used as a discriminate force and once again fit into the moral universe of just war constraints.

New capabilities raise new questions, of course. Regarding the use of newfound capabilities of airpower, questions arise concerning both the *jus in bello* and the *jus ad bellum* dimensions of just war thinking.

1. Competent militaries will certainly have anticipated disruption of basic infrastructure such as power grids and prepared workaround solutions to them. Given that reality, how do we make a reasonable assessment of the military "value at the time" of such dual use targets as electrical power in planning future air campaigns? The mere fact that it is reasonable to think that attack on such targets will achieve some military effect is not sufficient to meet the burden of proof that the civilian consequences are acceptable, legally and morally. The fact that coping with disruptions to normal services and infrastructure certainly will require diversion of personnel and resources from other military activities to some indeterminate degree is not, by itself, sufficient justification, either.

A calculation of proportionality requires at least a rough degree of quantification of these matters. We know pretty clearly the significant costs on the civilian side of the equation. It is important to ask for some equal attention to quantifying the military side of the ledger. For example, it is true that Iraqi air defenses were effectively neutralized early in the conflict. But it is also true that the absence of grid electrical power made a minor contribution at best to that neutralization. Far more important was the suppression of enemy air defenses by direct missile attack on targeting radars whenever they were engaged.

2. W. Hayes Parks is certainly correct when he suggests that Additional Protocol I to the Geneva Conventions of 1977 errs on

the side of assigning too much—indeed, nearly absolute—moral and legal responsibility for the welfare of civilians to the attacker. Clearly, there is a correlative responsibility of the defender to take reasonable precautions to separate civilian populations as much as possible from obvious military targets.[57] When an adversary such as Iraq routinely attempts to use the civilian population, civilian structures, and hostage foreign nationals and prisoners of war to shield military equipment and activity, such efforts cannot be given the approbation of international law.[58]

But destruction of basic civilian infrastructural elements is indeed primarily the responsibility of the attacker. A defender sincerely concerned with the welfare of its civilian populations might take care to segregate infrastructural elements into military and civilian categories in an effort to spare its population. It might declare and in good faith ensure (perhaps even inviting in neutral observers to verify) that some essential infrastructural elements are solely for civilian use. Still, it is unreasonable to ask that defenders segregate, say, civilian power grids from military ones. Indeed, in the absence of mutually trusted observers to verify such segregation, a defender's claim that it is doing so would hardly be credible.

But it is reasonable to require a good-faith effort on the part of the attacker to determine the genuine military necessity of attacks on targets with significant civilian value and use. Such a good-faith effort is necessary if one is to make a proportionality judgment of the "military value at the time" of attacks on such targets that err on the side of protecting civilian infrastructure.

3. Insofar as we wish to take the moral basis of noncombatant immunity seriously, how might we instrumentalize these considerations sufficiently to provide practical action-guidance to targeting staffs in future air war? At a minimum, might it not be worthwhile to collect and analyze a series of real cases of difficult targeting decisions for use in the training of targeters? Targeting staff officers should train routinely in making moral and legal as well as technical military judgments in war-gaming air campaigns.

4. The Gulf War and Kosovo disclosed even more sharply than ever before the interdependence of airpower effectiveness and intelligence, both in target identification and in bomb damage assessment.

Only insofar as theater commanders possess reliable target identification information can they successfully conduct air operations against truly essential military targets and diminish unnecessary disruption to civilian life and infrastructure. The promise of swift and simultaneous attack on centers of gravity that will rapidly remove an adversary's capacity to resist and wage war requires a level of understanding of both the military systems of the adversary and of the political context that remains elusive. At the level of strategic value, the "mistakes" in bombing the Chinese Embassy in Belgrade and the Al Firdos structure containing civilians in Baghdad clearly illustrate that even precision attack based on bad intelligence can threaten to unravel the strategic value of airpower.

Further, only insofar as bomb damage assessment is accurate and timely can unnecessary restriking of targets be avoided, further diminishing the risks to aircrews and the destruction of civilian life and property that is part of the friction of war.

5. The last and most perverse unintended consequence of the advance in airpower is on the *jus ad bellum* side of just war thinking. Kosovo seems to illustrate that the existence of the new technologies of air war (stealth, standoff munitions, and precision guidance combined) may serve to lower the threshold of the recourse to the use of military power. Rather than serving the just war requirement of last resort, the possession of capability to employ military means with impunity demonstrably tempts political leaders to use force rather than diplomacy to "send a message."

The moral foundation of the last resort requirement is the recognition that, because lives are placed at risk by military action, one should have recourse to it reluctantly and sparingly. Admittedly, the weight of human life is more palpable to political leaders when the lives in question are those of their own soldiers and citizens. But from the perspective of ethics, unequal weighting of the value of human life is impermissible, and the fact of virtual immunity of one's own military personnel engaged in military action does not in the least justify neglect of the lives of the adversary hazarded in the recourse to military force.

Nine

Transcending Westphalia

From 24 October 1945, the day the [United Nations] Charter entered into effect, it has had competition. Alongside it, and prefigured in the Charter itself, there ran a parallel legislative stream of humanitarian and human rights rules and standards which States undertook at least to take note of and which, if words mean anything, they should in some last resort be required to observe.... Members of the UN insist that they retain full sovereign rights, and nominally indeed they do so, yet they stand committed at the same time to a variety of human rights observances which in principle entitle their neighbours to complain in case of neglect.[1]

The decision to intervene in Kosovo was fraught with ironies. The most ardent advocates of the decision were, virtually without exception, civilian leaders who had a history of opposition to the Vietnam War and who were inexperienced in military realities. President Clinton, Secretary of State Albright, Strobe Talbot, Sandy Berger—every last person in the senior civilian leadership of the administration fit that profile.

In contrast, the military leadership of the nation, while officially supportive at the highest levels, was lukewarm at best in its enthusiasm for this use of military force. Military expert after military expert questioned the reliance on airpower alone as a strategy likely to succeed in Kosovo. Yet an equal lack of enthusiasm was apparent when the use of ground forces was suggested as an alternative.

Contrary to much expert military opinion, the airpower-only strategy (along with apparent withdrawal of support from the Russians) "succeeded." At least, it caused the Serbian leadership to withdraw from Kosovo. But it would be dangerous to conclude that this intervention was a success. At the level of military strategy—in terms of clear thinking about policy issues regarding the use of military force and in terms of the ethical issues involved in extended strategic bombing campaigns—the Kosovo intervention requires much examination before we can be sure what lessons are to be learned from it.

The differences between civilian and military thinking about the wisdom of the intervention in Kosovo stemmed from many sources. In part they rested on the more sober estimation of military capabilities by seasoned military leaders than by their civilian superiors. In part, they reflected the military's strong sense that it was being "stretched too thin." It was deployed all over the globe in various operations other than war, while struggling to recruit to a force already one-third smaller than the force that fought Desert Storm.

But there was a much deeper issue underlying these disagreements. Disagreements between the civilian leaders of the Clinton administration and the military thinking at the time pointed to profound and abiding questions of the purposes of the use of military force, of the relation of national militaries to sovereign states, and, of the meaningfulness of the idea of international community itself. It is precisely the disagreement the quotation from Geoffrey Best's magisterial *War and Law since 1945*, cited above, captures: between international order conceived on the paradigm of sovereign, independent states, and international order imagined as a defender of universal human rights and values.

The objections to the Kosovo intervention—both from the perspective of the United States and from Serbia, Russia, China, and many other states—rested on a view of international order and the use of military force that, as we have noted, stems from the Peace of Westphalia (1648). On that model, sovereign states possess territorial integrity and political sovereignty. This understanding generates what Michael Walzer has called a "legalist paradigm" as the standard case for thinking about military intervention, and rules out initiation of military conflict except in response to aggression.[2]

From the standard military perspective as well, military force exists to serve the interests of sovereign states. The decision to employ military power should be made only after careful and critical reflection that vital, or at least very important, national interests require action, and in particular the use of the blunt and costly instrument of military power. To this way of framing the problem, the wishes, desires, and even important values of the "international community" have nothing to do with the appropriate use of sovereign state power unless analysis of vital interests establishes a connection. It is universally agreed that Kosovo was a province of a sovereign state, and it was the stated policy of the United States (and others) to oppose any bid for the independence of Kosovo. No matter how tyrannical and oppressive that state may have been toward Kosovo, it was an internal matter for that state.

For the military forces of the United States, in particular, there was an additional stage of analysis before the decision to commit military forces was made. The gradual and ultimately ineffectual escalation of military force in Vietnam caused a soul-searching reconsideration of principles guiding the use of force on the part of the United States. The reconsideration culminated in the previously discussed Powell-Weinberger Doctrine—a virtual "creed" of United States military thinking. The central tenets of the creed are well known, and include the following. Military forces of the United States should not be committed unless there is a clearly defined national interest, achievable by use of military force, and specifiable in terms of a specific desired end-state. The cause to which military forces are to be committed must be unquestionably vital to national political interest and must have expectation of continuing support of the American people. Lastly, the forces committed to the operation must possess overwhelming capability in comparison to their opposition. Only such overwhelming force guarantees that the United States can avoid the kind of long and painful war of attrition and gradualism that Vietnam became.

Clearly, the Kosovo intervention was extremely difficult, if not impossible, to justify if one approaches it from either of these traditional moral and political perspectives. From the angle of the Westphalian legalist paradigm, it was unquestionably an intervention inside the territory of an internationally recognized sovereign state. As such, it falls far short of a response to international aggression, the sole legitimate cause for use of military force on the legalist paradigm model.

The Westphalian need not reject entirely a concern with the massive human rights violations in Kosovo in order to continue to reject intervention. In Best's words quoted above, other states "take note of" the violations, complain about them, cajole about them. But since the line between those verbal interferences in Yugoslav internal affairs and military intervention remains quite salient in international relations, such concerns do not add up to a *casus belli*.

Similarly, the military strategist need not be callous to the scenes of suffering in Kosovo, nor unwilling to join in the wish that "someone" would do "something" about it. Where the practical military strategist should hesitate is in moving from those moral sensibilities to operational military reality. The questions here were focused and practical: Given all the demands on a downsized force, was the interest in Kosovo "vital" enough to expend limited resources? Did it warrant stretching still further the deployment of soldiers, sailors, and airmen? Was the cause worth the risk of American life? Was the desired end-state clearly defined and achievable? Were the military strategy and forces committed to the standard of "overwhelming force" to assure success?

The Kosovo operation failed to meet the tests of either the Westphalian legalist model of international law or the hard-nosed practical standard of real-world military planning. In that light, it is not difficult to see why many non-NATO states failed to see the legal and moral justification of the operation, or why many leaders and members of the military deeply questioned the wisdom and prudence of the intervention.

This judgment remains vitally important, even though the Yugoslavs ultimately withdrew forces from Kosovo. Strategic decision-making is judged not by whether things merely happened to turn out as one wished, but by the quality of the thinking that went into deciding to intervene in the first place. And in this case, whether one views the decision through the lens of the Westphalian international system or of the Powell-Weinberger doctrine's view of the proper application of military force, the decision to initiate hostilities over Kosovo was unjustified and unwise.

It is not, however, this older and better-established body of law to which advocates of the Kosovo intervention appealed. The reformulated world system in years following World War II and the founding of the United Nations saw the birth of a new kind of universalism that, in principle at least, challenged the absolute state sovereignty of Westphalia. The Holocaust made graphically clear that the principle of state sovereignty must be limited to a degree and that human beings must be able to assert individual rights, even in the face of their governments. Without, perhaps, fully thinking through the consequences of their words, governments reacted to the horrors of genocide by committing themselves (on paper, anyway) to intervene in internal affairs of states when abuses of their citizens rise to the level of unacceptable.

This reaction began a process that has evolved a newer body of international law and moral thought (and with it spawned a proliferation of nongovernmental organizations concerned with them) that sits in imperfect harmony with the older system of state sovereignty. This newer system speaks of universal humanitarian responsibility of the international community and of universal human rights. As Best writes, "The wartime rhetoric which rushed them into commitment to post-war protection of human rights was tacked on to their political theory, not integrated into it."[3]

Universal human rights law and thought has the purpose of "averting or restricting the uses of violence by governments toward their own subjects," but it is "a field of conflict for which international law by definition brought no remedies."[4] The ringing language of humanitarian law left, unfortunately, a glaring contradiction with existing Westphalian sovereignty law: "[T]he concept of [humanitarian] intervention would still imply violating sovereign authority without having identified a higher authority on which the supremacy of human rights rests."[5] It is this declaration of moral and legal principle in the absence of clear delineation of authority that lies at the root of the ambiguity of justification of the Kosovo intervention. The principles are clearly stated, but the authority and military means to implement them are unclear. The United Nations Security Council, while ostensibly the nearest thing to universally valid legal authority, is rarely likely to find the political unanimity to enforce the principles (and certainly could not do so in Kosovo). NATO possesses the military means of enforcement and (just barely) the united political will to marshal it, but lacks even the appearance of universal legal authority.

Post–World War II humanitarian law drove the Kosovo intervention and, in the minds of its advocates, justified it legally and morally. Appealing to the morally compelling post-Holocaust proclamation "Never Again," the NATO allies attempted to make real a commitment that, at least in Europe itself, mass deportation and ethnically driven killing and persecution would not be permitted.

The use of NATO in service of this newer body of ostensibly universal law was a "road less taken" by major powers since World War II. Obviously, the fact that the intervention was NATO-authorized (rather than UN-sponsored) raised questions about the "universality" of its motives. While non-NATO powers may have viewed this rationale with cynicism or with alarm, in the minds of its advocates it was an affirmation of the use of military power for "idealistic" reasons. But the alarm was understandable as well in light of the precedent set by this action and the license it appeared to give for intervention in the name of humanitarian concerns.

Although national-interest arguments for the Kosovo intervention were offered, they failed to ring true, at least in regard to the motives of the United States.[6] The central motive was clearly humanitarian idealism that was prepared to pursue ideals apart from clear or narrowly conceived national interest. It was, to borrow a phrase, "humanitarian war"[7]—a concept poorly developed in theory, and rarely seen in practice. It was a war genuinely fought for principles of humanity. Unfortunately, "Humanity...is not a category for which we have prepared political concepts, despite the seeming internationalization of human rights and humanitarian discourse."[8]

The Kosovo intervention then pointed clearly to the divergence in two fundamentally different streams of international law and moral thought. The tension is pointedly illuminated in the following questions:

> Are human rights exclusively within the domestic jurisdiction of states or are they an international concern with community jurisdiction? ... Which authority is superior, state jurisdiction over individuals within its boundaries, or international jurisdiction over inalienable human rights?[9]

Conclusions

There are two areas where the Kosovo intervention raised important issues and questions for reflection and future precedent. One concerns the *jus ad bellum* justification for the intervention, and the other the *jus in bello* considerations raised by the extended strategic bombing campaign against Serbia.

On the *ad bellum* side, it is important to note the serious misfit between moral ideals (which surely press for defense of innocent victims of ethnic cleansing) and the limits of the presently possible in terms of international law and military power. No one of good will could resist the "something should be done about this" reaction to scenes of ethnic cleansing and murder in Kosovo. But the body of law that warranted intervention is recent and not well-integrated into the older system of state sovereignty.

While there may be an "international community" that is serious about intervening in Kosovo-like situations in the future, this intervention makes painfully clear that there is simply no effective international authority to provide legitimacy to such interventions. Except in the rare eventuality in which the permanent members of the Security Council concur, humanitarian war will be conducted unilaterally by single powers or by coalitions. Kosovo points clearly to the need to continue to work on structures of international political authority that can assess and authorize appropriate interventions.

The situation is similar on the military side. One can imagine only rare circumstances in which the military power of sovereign states will be provided to fight truly humanitarian war. As the "no ground war" announcements in Kosovo made very clear, leaders of states are loath to risk the lives of their nationals for a humanitarian cause—even if that is the price one has to pay to be militarily effective. Even with an "international community" committed to its espoused humanitarian values, new military structures will be needed to intervene effectively and decisively in such situations where the vital interests of sovereign states are marginally involved.

Lastly, there is a serious problem with the conduct of war in the Kosovo intervention. Precision-guided munitions make possible highly discriminate attacks on military targets and, barring failures of intelligence and equipment, go far toward eliminating civilian casualties as a direct result of bombing.[10] But what the Gulf War

foreshadowed rapidly became reality in the strategic bombing of
Serbia. An extended strategic bombing campaign, especially when a
follow-on ground campaign is ruled out from the beginning,
inevitably turns into a war against the fundamental infrastructure
of the opponent's society.

The Kosovo air campaign reached the point of serious disruption of the electrical and water systems of major Serbian cities. Had
it continued much longer, the "bomb now, die later" effects of infrastructure disruption would have become even more apparent and
widespread in their effects.

We have not yet begun to think seriously enough the moral
ambiguities of precision-guided munitions. Since air war has been, for
all its previous history, horribly indiscriminate, it is easy to be
impressed by the fact that direct targeting of civilians no longer takes
place. But already NATO's air campaign, frustrated that Serbia did
not immediately sue for peace after the attack on unambiguously military targets, had begun to create larger and larger circles of disruption of the fundamental societal infrastructure of Serbia.

We need to begin to come to terms with the moral limits of air
war conducted with precision guided missiles, just as we have
rethought the World War II tactic of area bombing and firebombing
of cities. Escalation of the target list in the determination to win a
war from the air can lead to civilian death and destruction on a
massive scale. Such civilian losses can occur even if civilians are
not directly bombed if they are deprived of the facilities that provide clean water and heat, medical care, and food. The bombing in
this case did result in troop withdrawal before we saw such effects
on a truly massive scale—but only just short of it. If we are going to
fight humanitarian wars, surely they must not be won over the
bodies of innocent civilians. If war fought to protect innocent civilians is to be won by destroying the lives of other innocent civilians,
the moral calculus is too difficult to reckon.

Notes

Introduction

1. All citations to Thucydides in this chapter are taken from *The Landmark Thucydides: A Comprehensive Guide to the Peloponnesian War*, ed. Robert B. Strassler (New York: Free Press, 1996).

2. See Donald Kagan, *The Outbreak of the Peloponnesian War* (Ithaca, NY: Cornell University Press, 1969), 37–38 for a discussion of Pausanias's conduct and character.

3. For a detailed discussion of the degree of organization and unity of the Spartan alliance, see ibid., 9–30.

4. Stanley Hoffman, "On the War," *New York Review of Books*, November 1, 2001.

5. See Kagan, *Outbreak*, 9–30, for abundant evidence of Sparta's inability to rely on alliance support for operations.

6. See ibid., 118–19.

7. See ibid., 251–72, for a full discussion of the vexed historical question here.

8. Ibid., 140: "Now every one of the Allies has to cringe to the Attic people ... and in court anybody is obliged to beseech and stretch out his hand to the casual person entering. Consequently the allies have more and more been made slaves of the people of Athens."

9. Kagan argues that there was a version of Panhellenism advocated by Pericles' opponents that would have upheld the equality of all Greek states. He associates this position with the views of the Greek aristocracy throughout the Greek world—perhaps the analogue to the views of internationalist intellectuals who see identity in larger terms than that of individual states? See ibid., 159. Kagan further argues that Athens did have a real strategic option short of inevitable war with Sparta and her allies. He attempts to show that, for a period at least, there was a de facto "spheres of influence" stability in which Corinth recognized the freedom of Athens to act with a free hand with her own subordinate

159

states and expected equal freedom in her own sphere. On this analysis, the affair at Corcyra was a breach of that tacit understanding (see ibid., 174).

10. I borrow the helpful distinction between being imperial and being imperialist from Richard N. Haass, "Imperial Understretch," *Hoover Digest*, no. 3, 2000.

11. Ibid.

12. Paul Kennedy, *The Rise and Fall of Great Powers* (London: Hyman, 1988).

13. Cassandra was, of course, the Trojan woman cursed by the gods to always accurately foretell the future, but never to be listened to.

14. I do not by any means think that the American objections to the court and the Rome Treaty are completely mistaken. My point is that we seem to be attempting to craft for American forces an absolute exemption from its jurisdiction. Instead, we might more effectively lead in creating an institution with proper definitions of crime and with sufficient jurisdiction to make the leap to a new international recognition of moral principle.

Chapter 2

1. William James, "The Moral Equivalent of War," in *War and Morality*, Richard Wasserstrom, ed. (Belmont, CA: Wadsworth Publishing Co., 1970), 7.

2. Michael Walzer, *Just and Unjust Wars: A Moral Argument with Historical Illustrations*, 2nd ed. (New York: Basic Books, 1977), 12.

3. Carl von Clausewitz, *On War*, book 1, chapter 1, sec. 23.

4. Augustine, *The City of God*, book 4, sec. 4.

5. Ibid.

6. Augustine, *Confessions*, book 1, chapter 1, sec. 1.

7. James Bond Stockdale, "The World of Epictetus: Reflections on Survival and Leadership," in *War, Morality, and the Military Profession* (2nd ed., revised and updated), Malham M. Wakin, ed. (Boulder, CO: Westview Press, 1986), 10–22.

8. Dwight D. Eisenhower, *Crusade in Europe* (New York: 1948), 156–57, quoted in Walzer, *Just and Unjust Wars*, 37.

9. Walzer, *Just and Unjust Wars*, 54.

10. Ibid.

11. Nelson Mandela, "Address by Nelson Mandela, President of the Republic of South Africa, before a Joint Meeting of the United States Congress," Oct. 6, 1994. *Congressional Record—House* H11008.

Chapter 3

1. For representative samples among the sea of articles making these points, see Justin Brown, "Low Morale Saps United States Military Might," *Christian Science Monitor*, September 8, 2000, 30 and Fred Reed, "Military Service Warning Labels," *Washington Times*, September 10, 2000.

2. Don M. Snider, John A. Nagl, and Tony Pfaff, *Army Professionalism, Military Ethics, and Officership in the 21st Century* (Carlisle Barracks, PA: Army War College Strategic Studies Institute, 1999).

3. See Leonard Wong, *Generations Apart: Xers and Boomers in the Officer Corps* (Carlisle Barracks, PA: Army War College Strategic Studies Institute, 2000).

4. Eliot Friedson, *Professionalism Reborn: Theory, Policy and Prophecy* (Chicago: University of Chicago Press, 1994), 124. It is interesting to note that exactly the sort of institutional context Friedson's analysis offers is also part of Snider and Watkin's analysis of the army's present situation. They write, "[T]here is a gross mismatch between institutional capabilities and national needs." Don M. Snider and Gayle Watkins, "The Future of Army Professionalism: A Need for Renewal and Redefinition," *Parameters* [30, no. 3 (Autumn 2000): 8.

5. Charles C. Moskos, "Toward a Postmodern Military: The United States as a Paradigm," in *The Postmodern Military: Armed Forces after the Cold War*, ed. Charles C. Moskos, John Allen Williams, and David R. Segal (New York: Oxford University Press, 2000), 14–31.

6. Andrew Abbott, *The System of Professions: An Essay on the Division of Expert Labor* (Chicago: University of Chicago Press, 1988).

7. This is, of course, the basic thrust of the analysis offered in Snider, Nagl and Pfaff.

8. Ibid., 21.

9. Friedson, *Professionalism Reborn*, 210.

10. Snider and Watkins, *Parameters* [XXX, n. 3, Autumn, 2000], 7.11. To further illustrate this misunderstanding: suppose one were to say that because physicians serve patients and the health of the society more generally, it would be unprofessional of them to assert intellectual independence and superior knowledge of medicine. Clearly, it is only insofar as physicians do possess intellectual independence and superior knowledge that they are of any use to the society as doctors. To say that, however, is not to say that society does not have the right to limit the discretion of physicians to use that expertise as they see fit. Society may well (for example) rule out medical procedures that are medically indicated if they are too expensive from the perspective of public policy. In that case, the physician would have to decide whether to provide a less expensive alternative procedure, even

though it might be less desirable from a narrowly medical perspective. Presumably, at some point resources could be so limited that the physician would feel it would be "unprofessional" to continue to practice medicine in such an environment.

11. To further illustrate this misunderstanding: suppose one were to say that because physicians serve patients and the health of the society more generally, it would be unprofessional of them to assert intellectual independence and superior knowledge of medicine. Clearly, it is only insofar as physicians do possess intellectual independence and superior knowledge that they are of any use to the society as doctors. To say that, however, is not to say that society does not have the right to limit the discretion of physicians to use that expertise as they see fit. Society may well (for example) rule out medical procedures that are medically indicated if they are too expensive from the perspective of public policy. In that case, the physician would have to decide whether to provide a less expensive alternative procedure, even though it might be less desirable from a narrowly medical perspective. Presumably, at some point resources could be so limited that the physician would feel it would be "unprofessional" to continue to practice medicine in such an environment.

12. Friedson, *Professionalism Reborn*, 211.

13. H. R. McMaster, *Dereliction of Duty: Johnson, McNamara, the Joint Chiefs of Staff and the Lies That Led to Vietnam* (New York: HarperCollins, 1997).

14. Needless to say, one can imagine some scenario in which trash collection or guarding school crossings becomes a critical social need. In that situation, one might well appeal to physicians to assist in those activities. But one would be appealing to them as citizens, or as benevolent individuals, not because of any obligation inherent in their professional status. If they are employees of an organization, one might even require such service of them in the exigency of the moment. But even in that case, they would not be rendering service *as professionals*, but rather merely as able-bodied employees.

15. Friedson, *Professionalism Reborn*, 211.

16. The term is from Snider and Watkins, "Future of Army Professionalism," 7.

17. An interesting historical question arises that I am not competent to address: To what extent did experienced combat leaders following the Civil War experience a similar professional disorientation when they were tasked with garrisoning the West and with national development missions in the late nineteenth century?

18. Friedson, *Professionalism Reborn*, 122–123.

19. Edwin Dorn, Howard D. Graves, Walter F. Ulmer, Joseph J. Collins, and T. O. Owens, *American Military Culture in the Twenty-First Century: A Report of the*

CSIS *International Security Program* (Washington, DC: Center for Strategic and International Studies, 2000).

20. See Wong, *Generations Apart*, for a full discussion of these issues.

21. Geoffrey Perret, *Eisenhower* (New York: Random House, 1999), 88.

22. United States Military Academy, *United States Military Academy Strategic Vision—2020* (West Point, N.Y.: United States Military Academy, 2000), 4.

23. Martin L. Cook, "'Immaculate War': Constraints on Humanitarian Intervention," *Ethics and International Affairs* 14 (2000), 55–65.

24. See James Kitfield, *Prodigal Soldiers* (New York: Simon and Schuster, 1995), for a detailed account of the much-eroded state of military professionalism in the aftermath of the Vietnam War and of the reforms then instituted to increase the effectiveness and professionalism of the army. This is significant, because it is precisely the culture and institutions created by those reforms that are now threatened by the challenges of the current situation.

25. See Suzanne C. Nielsen, "Rules of the Game: The Weinberger Doctrine and the American Use of Force," in *The Future of the Army Profession*, ed. Don M Snider and Gayle L. Watkins (Boston: McGraw-Hill Primus Custom Publishing, 2002), for a full development of this argument.

26. See Douglas V. Johnson and Leonard Wong, "A Historical Look at the Army Profession," in Snider and Watkins, *Future of the Army Profession*.

27. This was written before the attacks of September 11, 2001. Afghanistan showed the need for a much different force structure and use of forces than the cold war configuration. The 2003 war in Iraq, however, vindicated the need for heavy armored forces in some combat scenarios, while also in the aftermath showing the need for forces better prepared for civil affairs, psychological operations units, and other components of peacekeeping and nation building. The point of these observations is that the intellectual component of the professional consists precisely in thinking through the rapidly changing environment of the profession and adapting the professional knowledge and practice to remain as relevant as possible to that fluid environment. The tensions one hears reported between the civilian leadership of the Department of Defense and some of its uniformed leadership clearly reflect a suspicion (fair or unfair) on the part of the civilians that that kind of intellectual agility is lacking among the uniformed leaders.

Chapter 4

1. Snider, Nagl and Pfaff, *Army Professionalism*. These authors argue that the posture of "radical force protection" adopted by the US Army in Balkan peacekeeping deployments is evidence of a diminished sense of professional responsibility in the officer corps.

2. For a full and painstaking articulation of those realities in the Balkan conflicts, see Wesley K. Clark, *Waging Modern War* (New York: Public Affairs, 2001).

3. The general question of the state of military professionalism and of the scope and limits of professional military advice is receiving considerable discussion in the contemporary literature. Many of the essays in Snider and Watkins, *Future of the Army Profession*, address this question explicitly. See in particular the essays by James Burk, Suzanne Nielsen, and Martin L. Cook. Thomas Ricks, the Pentagon reporter for the *Washington Post*, has recently written a novel, *A Soldier's Duty* (New York: Random House, 2001), that dramatizes the tensions he feels are emerging in those relationships and the temptation of military officers to subvert constitutional authority to prevent what, in the novel, the military views as misguided uses of military force by the civilian leadership.

4. Suzanne Nielsen's excellent discussion of this point in "Rules of the Game: The Weinberger Doctrine and American Use of Force" in Snider and Watkins, *Future of the Army Profession*, 199–224.

5. See James Kitfield, *Prodigal Soldiers* (Westinghouse Brassey's, 1997), for a detailed account of these reform efforts and how their success has both permeated contemporary military culture and enabled the military to fight effectively in Desert Storm.

6. Ricks's novel *A Soldier's Duty* graphically illustrates the depths of frustration and disillusionment experienced in the ranks by such assignments. It is, in my judgment, an only slight exaggerated portrayal of the cultural reality.

7. See Douglas V. Johnson and Leonard Wong, "A Historical Look at the Army Profession," in Snider and Watkins, *Future of the Army Profession*.

8. See Martin L. Cook, "Army Professionalism: Service for What Ends?" in Snider and Watkins, *Future of the Army Profession*, 337–54.

9. Clark, *Waging Modern War*, 125.

10. The phrase was coined by Professor George Lucas of the United States Naval Academy. See George R. Lucas, *Perspectives on Humanitarian Military Intervention* (Berkeley, CA: Public Policy Press, Institute of Government Studies, and University of California Press, 2001).

11. Rather typical is this short note: "Majr. Genl. McClellan, I have just read your despatch [*sic*] about sore tongued and fatiequed [*sic*] horses. Will you pardon me for asking what the horses of your army have done since the battle of Antietam that fatigue anything?" *Lincoln: Speeches, Letters, Miscellaneous Writings and Presidential Messages and Proclamations, 1859–1865* (New York: Library of America, 1989), 379–80.

12. Snider, Nagl and Pfaff, *Army Professionalism*.

13. Michael Ignatieff, *Virtual War: Kosovo and Beyond* (New York: Metropolitan Books, 2000).

14. This issue was routinely illustrated in my elective course at the US Army War College. As we work through Michael Walzer's *Just and Unjust Wars*, we get to the section where he discusses the traditional moral principle of double effect as it applies to combat operations. Walzer modifies the conventional formulation somewhat to include the notion that soldiers must accept risk to themselves to err in favor of protection of innocent life. The example I offered to my class was this: "Suppose you are advancing in an armored column toward a small village and receive small-arms fire from one or two weapons. What should you do?" In one offering of this course, one student, an armor lieutenant colonel and former battalion commander, offered the opinion that there was only one tactically correct solution to this situation: turn the turrets of all the tanks in the column on the village and open fire. When I suggested that it might be the case that only a couple of individuals in the village were offering resistance and that their small-arms fire was ineffective anyway against armor, he dismissed those concerns and indicated that his instructions were to always open fire with everything he had until the opposition ceased. Was there a good chance innocents would be killed by this approach? Yes, but in his view, it was acceptable collateral damage. I would add that this officer is well known to me personally, and is generally an outstanding and very thoughtful military professional. I cite the example not in any way as a criticism of him personally. Rather, I take it as an indication of the pervasiveness of this kind of thinking that even an officer of his caliber would be culturally averse to any other approach

Chapter 5

1. "We do not all agree with Michael Smith's affirmation of humanitarian intervention, but we think it should be included." Glen Stassen, ed., *Just Peacemaking: Ten Practices for Abolishing War* (Cleveland: Pilgrim Press, 1998), 26.

2. Paul Schroeder's contribution to the volume is the most nuanced in its analysis of the international situation. Unlike many of the other articles, it does not so much see an inevitable evolution of the international system in a single direction as a tension between competing models, each of which is focused on different constellations of values. His claims are quite modest: that just peacemaking "strategies and tactics can work far more widely and durably than they used to, or than many think; that where they do not work, often nothing else will work either; and that plenty of evidence from recent peacekeeping and peacebuilding illustrates their value." Paul Schroeder "Work with Emerging Cooperative Forces in the International System," in Stassen, *Just Peacekeeping*, 143–44.

3. This is stated perhaps even more strongly in the Cartright and Thistlethwaite essay: "Citizens and governments must support and work with such campaigns in situations of actual or potential conflict before the condition of 'last resort' can be employed to justify violence. Hence the practice of nonviolent direct action is an obligatory norm where nonviolently it can transform festering injustice into constructive change," John Cartwright and Susan Thirtlewaite "Support Nonviolent Direct Action." This assertion is, of course, ambiguous, if not confused, on the character of the "oughts" it is asserting. The first sentence asserts as

an absolute principle that nonviolent means must always be tried before the last-resort principle can legitimately be satisfied. The second sentence makes the requirement conditional: it is a norm "where . . . it can transform. . . ." This seems to suggest the more reasonable view that one may make a good faith judgment whether, in a given situation, nonviolent means are likely to be effective.

4. Michael Smith is well aware of the problem. He writes, "This process [of approving interventions] should, in my view, be multinational. For all the flaws of the United Nations, it does provide a forum for international debate and for the emergence of consensus. And insistence on collective, multilateral intervention—or, as in Haiti, collectively approved unilateral action—can correct for self-interested interventions thinly cloaked in humanitarianism. At the same time, it may be just or necessary for a state to declare its intention to act on its own." Michael Joseph Smith "Strengthen the United Nations and International Efforts for Cooperation and Human Rights." This states the problem accurately, but with a bit more confidence in the power of consensus to emerge than I believe experience warrants.

5. Even that presents far more complications than may be obvious. The NATO intervention in Kosovo was clearly a humanitarian intervention. NATO is the best integrated and prepared military alliance in human history, yet even NATO found it almost impossible, to maintain enough unity of command and effort to conduct the mission successfully. Even a cursory reading of Clark, *Waging Modern War*, ought to give serious pause to anyone advocating that NATO conduct another such mission—let alone that the UN try it. Also, few regional powers have the kinds of well-disciplined forces one may really want to unleash, even if with multinational authority: witness the conduct of the Nigerian forces in Sierra Leone.

6. Some significant alternative perspectives include Benjamin R. Barber, *Jihad vs. McWorld: How Globalism and Tribalism Are Reshaping the World* (New York: Ballantine Books, 1995); Samuel P. Huntington, *The Clash of Civilizations and the Remaking of World Order* (New York: Touchstone, 1996); John Lewis Gaddis, "Living in Candlestick Park," *Atlantic Monthly*, April 1999; and Michael Ignatieff, *Blood and Belonging: Journeys into the New Nationalism* (New York: Farrar, Straus and Giroux, 1994).

7. Donald Kagan and Frederick W. Kagan, *While America Sleeps: Self-Delusion, Military Weakness, and the Threat to Peace Today* (New York: St. Martin's Press, 2000). I have attempted to provide a parallel, but somewhat more internationalist, vision in the introductory chapter to this volume.

8. As a practical matter, I very much doubt the feasibility of an effective military force under UN control for any but the first of Smith's three categories of international forces (Michael Joseph Smith "Strengthen the United Nations and International Efforts for Cooperation and Human Rights," 152–52). Even peace-enforcement, not to mention genuine war-fighting, requires a level of training, interoperable equipment, operational security, unity of command and control, and

so on, that is difficult for a single state to attain. It would be challenging for any coalition and I suspect impossible unless and until the UN truly serves as a world government rather than as a loose coalition of states. For that reason, I find even Smith's contribution to the JP project utopian—and it is the most realistic.

9. A very important contribution to this question has been made recently by the "Brahimi Report" to the United Nations (http://www.un.org/peace/reports/peace_operations/). This report and the various responses to it (also available on the UN's website) very critically assess the strengths and limitations of historic UN peacekeeping operations and make important and constructive suggestions about how the UN's ability to conduct such operations might be dramatically improved.

10. Ibid.

11. http://www.fema.gov/rrr

Chapter 6

1. *City of God*, 19.

2. *Leviathan*, 13.62

Chapter 7

1. Harvey Sapolsky and Jeremy Shapiro, "Administration Deft to Predict Public Fatigue for a Longer War," *Army Times*, October 18, 1999.

2. Geoffrey Best, *War and Law since 1945* (Oxford: Clarendon Press, 1994), 79.

3. PDD-25 (unclassified version), Glenn Bowens, in *Legal Guide to Peace Operations* (Carlisle Barracks, PA: US Army Peacekeeping Institute, 1998), 358.

4. PDD-56 (unclassified version), in Bowens, *Legal Guide to Peace Operations*, 372.

5. Ibid.

6. Ibid.

7. UN Press Release SG/SM/7136, GA/95/96.

8. Ibid.

9. Ibid.

10. Ibid.

11. PDD-25 (unclassified version), in Bowen *Legal Guide to Peace Operations*, 363–64.

12. Ibid., 365.

13. See Martin L. Cook, "Moral Foundations of Military Service," *Parameters* (Spring 2000).

14. Wesley Clark, "The United States and NATO: The Way Ahead," *Parameters*, 29, no. 4 (Winter 1999-2000): 2–14.

15. Earl H. Tilford, Jr., "Operation Allied Force and the Role of Air Power," *Parameters*, 29, no. 4 (Winter 1999–2000), 29.

Chapter 8

1. Of course, each of these weapons systems had been employed to some degree in earlier conflicts. Precision guided munitions had been used in Vietnam for instance, and F-117s saw some action in Panama. Still, "debut" seems an appropriate use here in that, for the first time, these systems were employed in large quantities and in pursuit of an integrated strategy.

2. For a detailed discussion of the evolution of the technology and strategic thinking regarding air power, see Benjamin S. Lambeth, *The Transformation of American Air Power* (Ithaca: Cornell University Press, 2000). See also Robert A. Pape, *Bombing to Win: Air Power and Coercion in War* (Ithaca: Cornell University Press, 1996) for a detailed analysis of the uses of airpower historically and their efficacy.

3. See *Gulf War Air Power Survey, v. II* (Washington: Government Printing Office, 1993), 348-370 (hereafter GWAPS) for a detailed discussion of whether the Gulf War is a "revolution in military affairs."

4. Michael Sherry, *The Rise of American Airpower: The Creation of Armageddon* (New Haven: Yale University Press, 1989), 2.

5. Ibid., 5.

6. Ibid., 19.

7. Quoted in ibid., 25.

8. Quoted in ibid., 25.

9. Sherry, 53.

10. See ibid., 99–100.

11. Ibid., 256–300. Sherry uses this point as support of the thesis that the Air Corps of World War II was totally in the thrall of the ideal of terror bombing. Dr. Thomas Keaney helpfully points out that the B-29s were, in fact, designed for strategic bombing. The strategic theory of the time made it seem to the planners that diverting their efforts toward sea lanes would be a misuse of the weapons system and would prevent their efficient fulfillment of the goal of crippling Japan

and ending the war without the need for an invasion. That such models were correct seems, in hindsight, unlikely.

12. James L. Stokesbury, *A Short History of Airpower* (New York: William Morrow, 1986), 190.

13. *Air Force Manual 1-1, vol. 2, Basic Aerospace Doctrine of the United States* (1992), 148.

14. Best, *War and Law since 1945,* 200.

15. Quoted in ibid., 200.

16. Ibid., 204.

17. Private communication. Lt. Col. William G. Schmidt, USAF, United States Air Force Academy, Department of Law.

18. ICRC, "Summary of the Geneva Conventions," 17.

19. Ibid., 17.

20. W. Hayes Parks, "Air Power and the Law of War," *The Air Force Law Review 32(1),* 113. Parks very extensively and helpfully analyzes the difficulties with the language of Protocol I in five areas: (1) the definition of "attack," (2) the definitions of "civilian" and "combatant," (3) the definition of military object, (4) the apparent equation in value of civilian life and civilian property, and (5) the weight of responsibility for civilian welfare assigned to attacker and to defender. For our purposes, this level of detail is not important. What is important is the clear and agreed-upon prohibition of indiscriminate bombing.

21. Michael Walzer makes a complex and interesting argument in favor of area bombing in the very early phases of the war (see *Just and Unjust* Wars, 255–63 for this discussion). He argues that military necessity made such attacks acceptable during the small window of time when it was the only practical means to attack Germany. Whatever one thinks of this argument, however, he agrees as well that the justification for area bombing ceased fairly quickly when other means became available.

22. *Air Force Manual 1-1, vol. 2* (1992), 5–3 a.1.a.

23. However, for a much grimmer assessment of the future value of such weapons, see Col. Charles J. Dunlap, Jr.'s provocative piece, "How We Lost the High-Tech War of 2007," *The Weekly Standard* (29 January, 1996), 22-28.

24. Rick Atkinson, *Crusade: the Untold Story of the Persian Gulf* War (Boston: Houghton Mifflin, 1999), 56.

25. John A. Warden, *The Air Campaign: Planning for Combat* (Washington: National Defense University Press, 1988), 4.

26. Atkinson, *Crusade,* 58.

27. Quoted in ibid., 59.

28. Ibid., 63.

29. E.g., *Air Force Manual 1–1, vol. 2.*

30. Ibid., 151.

31. Ibid., 152.

32. Warden, *The Air Campaign,* 8.

33. *Air Force Manual 1–1, vol.2, 148.*

34. Ibid.

35. Ibid., 158.

36. *Air Force Doctrine Document 2–1.2,* "Strategic Attack" (May 20, 1998), p. 13, all emphasis original.

37. Ibid., p. 15

38. *Air Force Doctrine Document 2–1,* "Air Warfare" (22 January 2000), p. 11. For current doctrine statements, see also *Air Force Doctrine Document 2–1.2,* "Strategic Attack" (30 September 2003) and *Air Force Doctrine Document 2,* "Organization and Employment of Aerospace Power" (17 February 2000). All current doctrine documents are available via website at the USAF Doctrine Center: https://www.doctrine.af.mil

39. See GWAPS: Summary Report, chapter 10 for a nuanced discussion of this claim.

40. *Needless Deaths in the Gulf War: Civilian Casualties during the Air Campaign and Violations of the Laws of War* (New York: Human Rights Watch, 1991), 17–20.

41. GAO/PEMD-96-10.

42. It is important to note that there is always tension between the desire to protect one's own troops and the development of weaponry. For example, laser-guided munitions, which clearly make possible highly accurate bombing, also require pilots to fly straight and level in order to hold the laser designator on the target. This requires pilots to forego the kind of evasive maneuvers they would normally commence immediately after release of more traditional bombs.

43. See GAO/NSIAD–97–134, 40–41 for specific GAO analysis of these shortcomings. See also Lambeth, *Transformation of American Air Power,* for a detailed technical discussion of the nature and scope of those improvements.

44. GAO, *PEMD–96–10*, 4

45. It is important to note that "Contrary to the general public's impression about the use of guided munitions in Desert Storm, . . . approximately 95 percent of the total bombs delivered against strategic targets were *unguided*; 5 percent were guided. Unguided bombs accounted for over 90 percent of both total bombs and bomb tonnage. Approximately 92 percent of the total tonnage was unguided, compared to 8 percent guided" (GAO/NSIAD–97–134, 69). Given these numbers, the lack of significant civilian collateral damage is extraordinary—perhaps an artifact of the location of many strategic targets in Iraq away from population centers? The accuracy of weapons delivery from the F-117 Stealth was also overplayed considerably in the popular media. See the detailed analysis of the accuracy of F-117 bombing at GAO/NSIAD–97–134, 127–43. In general, this study shows that there were considerable numbers of bomb misses—counting as "misses" anything from 3.2 meters to 178.1 meters from aim points. This moderates considerably the expectation of certain destruction of targets through the use of guided munitions in future conflicts. On the other hand, this is an improvement by several orders of magnitude in the distance of misses, compared to World War II or even Vietnam—a fact that is important when one focuses on civilian collateral damage. That is, even if targets were not destroyed by such weapons, at least the bombs seem largely to have fallen in the immediate target area rather than far afield, where the probability of damage to civilian life and property would be considerably higher.

46. See GAO/NSIAD–97–134, 123 for a detailed analysis of the degree to which this "one bomb, one target" goal was not attained. The main conclusion was that "the average number of LGBS [laser guided bombs] dropped per target was four."

47. Clark, *Waging Modern War* (New York: Public Affairs, 2001), 59–84. I am entirely sympathetic to Clark's concern and insistence that a great deal of care needs to be taken in future conflicts to make good faith judgments of the relative military value of such targets in comparison to the costs to civilian populations. I do not agree, however, that international law is, as yet, very clear on this point—and certainly not that we can with any confidence refer to the infrastructure destruction in the Gulf War as "war crimes."

48. Ibid., 62–63.

49. GWAPS, *Summary Report*, 71.

50. GWAPS, *Summary Report*, 73.

51. *Harvard Study Team Report: Public Health in Iraq after the Gulf War*, May 1991, 12–13; quoted in GWAPS, *Summary Report*, 75.

52. Beth Osborne Daponte, "Iraqi Casualties from the Persian Gulf War and Its Aftermath," quoted in GWAPS, *Summary Report*, 75.

53. GWAPS, *Summary Report*, 74.

54. Ibid., 75. See also p. 75, footnotes 44–45 for additional citations on point.

55. Clark, *Waging Modern War* (Cambridge, MA: Perseus Book Group, 2001), pp. 192–220 for a full and painful description of the inner working of the air campaign.

56. Timothy J. Sakulich, "Precision Engagement at the Strategic Level of War: Guiding Promise or Wishful Thinking?" Occasional Paper 25 (Maxwell AFB, AL: Center for Strategy and Technology, Air War College, December, 2001).

57. W. Hayes Parks, "Air Power and the Law of War," 156.

58. This lack of balanced assessment in the responsibilities of both attackers and defenders is one of the major flaws in the critique offered by Ramsey Clark and other extreme critics. While they are right to document the destruction of the war, they are often lacking in evenhanded assessment of the moral and legal responsibilities of the parties.

Chapter 9

1. Best, *War and Law since 1945*, 79.

2. Walzer, *Just and Unjust Wars:* 58-63.

3. Best, *War and Law since 1945*, 68.

4. Ibid., 69.

5. Jarat Chopra and Thomas G. Weiss, "Sovereignty Is No Longer Sacrosanct: Codifying Humanitarian Intervention," *Ethics and International Affairs* 6 (1992): 111.

6. The situation appears quite different from a European perspective. And clearly what the whole course of the Balkans conflict has painfully revealed is the lack of an indigenous European military and political capability to deal with European problems without direct US participation and leadership.

7. The phrase is from Adam Roberts, "Humanitarian War: Military Intervention and Human Rights," *International Affairs* 69 (1993): 429–49

8. Amir Pasic and Thomas G. Weiss, "The Politics of Rescue: Yugoslavia's Wars and the Humanitarian Impulse," *Ethics and International Affairs* 11 (1997): 126.

9. Chopra and Weiss, "Sovereignty," 109.

10. Martin L. Cook, "Applied Just War Theory: Moral Implications of New Weapons for Air War," *Annual of the Society of Christian Ethics* (1998): 199-219.

Index